STOP
CIRCLING

DEBORAH JOHNSON

STOP CIRCLING

STEPS TO ESCAPE ENDLESS ROUNDABOUTS

Stop Circling: Steps to Escape Endless Roundabouts

Copyright © 2023 Deborah Johnson

All rights reserved. No parts of this book may be used or reproduced by any means, graphic, electronic or mechanical, including photocopying, recording, taping, or by any information storage retrieval system without the written permission of the publisher except in the case of brief quotations embodied in critical articles and reviews.

Johnson, Deborah, author

Issued in print and electronic format
ISBN: 978-1-7333484-6-1 (hardback)
ISBN: 978-1-7333484-5-4 (paperback)
ISBN: 978-1-7333484-7-8 (ebook)

Because of the dynamic nature of the Internet, any web addresses or links obtained in this book may have changed since publication and may no longer be valid.

Cover Design by Wordzworth Books, © Deborah Johnson
• Commercial permission

Logo Meghanshu Sharma (Ingeniousart) © Deborah Johnson
• Commercial permission

Deborah's photo by Samir Janjua • Commercial permission

Visit Deborah's websites at: *DeborahJohnsonSpeaker.com; GoalsForYourLife.com; DJWorksMusic.com*

Hero Mountain®, Roundabout Hero™, HALFERS Tool™
are a Registered Trademarks, All Rights Reserved

Dedicated to all those who are circling, yet have so much to give.
Our world needs you.

Acknowledgements

It is difficult to acknowledge all who continue to inspire me and have an impact on my life. Much of the inspiration for this book came from developing a new keynote speech with my Heroic Public Speaking colleagues and Michael and Amy Port. Jen Singer, also known as "Macheté Jen," was the HPS coach who helped identify the stickiness of a roundabout in my talk. Through many Zoom rehearsals with others, the messaging was refined and ultimately, expanded. I am extremely grateful for the growth I experienced through the process.

My special thanks to Betsy Jackson who helped me develop the articles which provided the bones of this book. And to my good friend who has been by my side in most all my writing projects, Paula Miller. Your editing expertise as well as friendship are so very valuable in my life. You have been honest, yet affirming for me as I have grown through the writing of each book I have penned. I still have much to learn, but with the right team around me, I know the thoughts in my head will continue to be voiced. There are many others who have encouraged me, including my musician friends and lifetime group. I am rich because of the relationships I have in my life.

My own family is at the top of my grateful list. To our sons, Mike, Dan and Dave, I am so proud and full of joy at the men you have become. You are all so different, yet so alike. Now, you each are growing your own families with women I pray for daily. My prayers include the hope that you will continue to enjoy each other as much Greg and I have in raising you and that you'd create memories with your families that are long-lasting.

STOP CIRCLING

Greg, we continue to grow even closer through this stage of our lives and I cherish our times together. The cappuccinos you make me every morning along with our conversations have grown richer through the years. As we watch the lines on both of our faces grow deeper, I am glad we are still in this journey together after over 40 years. We have each gone through our own personal roundabouts, but with a united purpose, we have been able to exit successfully time and again. Ringing true in my heart are the well-known lyrics of the song I have not only performed, but continue to enjoy, "I will always love you."

Contents

Acknowledgements		vii
Introduction		xi
Part 1	**Position**	**1**
Chapter 1	The Roundabout	3
Chapter 2	The Assessment	5
Chapter 3	Halfers Tool	7
Chapter 4	How to Evaluate	10
Chapter 5	Determining Current Position: Health, Attitude, Learning, and Finances	13
Chapter 6	Determining Current Position: Employment, Relationships, and Spirituality	17
Chapter 7	The First Steps	22
Chapter 8	The Next Steps	26
Part 1	**Perspective**	**33**
Chapter 9	Perspective with Objectivity	35
Chapter 10	Perspective with Mindsets	37
Chapter 11	Perspective with a New Light	43
Chapter 12	Perspective from Others	45
Chapter 13	Perspective from Input	47
Chapter 14	Perspective from Accountability	50
Chapter 15	Others' Perspectives	53
Chapter 16	Self-Perspective	56
Chapter 17	Staying on Track	60
Part 1	**Purpose**	**65**
Chapter 18	Purpose vs. Mission	67
Chapter 19	Benefits of Purpose	69

Chapter 20	Why is Purpose Important for Us?	73
Chapter 21	Discovering Our Purpose	76
Chapter 22	Taking Action	81
Chapter 23	Why Dig Deeper?	83
Chapter 24	How to Dig Deeper	88
Part 1	**Exercises and Journal Prompts**	91
Chapter 25	Position Exercise — Part 1	92
Chapter 26	Position Exercise — Part 2	106
Chapter 27	Perspective Exercise — Part 1	110
Chapter 28	Perspective Exercise — Part 2	115
Chapter 29	Perspective Exercise — Part 3	120
Chapter 30	Purpose Exercise — Part 1	123
Chapter 31	Purpose Exercise — Part 2	126

Appendix — 133
About the Author — 143
Endnotes — 145

Introduction

I had not planned to write another book so soon after releasing my previous book *The Summit*. In fact, I was gathering ideas for a second allegorical tale in my *Summit* book series. However, while speaking at events and in my podcast about the difficulty of exiting a roundabout and feeling stuck, the topic of an endless roundabout resonated with my audiences. It also resonated with me. For many were finding themselves still spinning after shutdowns, from shifts in the economy, and from mandates that interrupted their lives. They could not think about climbing their professional summits until they could exit their constant spinning to find a more normal course, or the now-called "new normal."

However, this post-pandemic period still didn't feel normal—not to others nor to me. After publishing several articles on this topic of adjusting to adversity, the growing need to help other professionals became the foundation of this book. I decided that you, the audience, matter enough to finish it.

My purpose in writing is to create a simple system that can be applied and reapplied to give others a clear path for a successful exit from multiple roundabouts, where we inevitably find ourselves circling needlessly. It may feel risky to go through the steps to create the self-recognition needed for change and growth, but it is worth it, whether as an individual or team. The journal exercises and prompts contained in the following chapters are formatted specifically to help readers easily document their assessment, thoughts, and responses.

STOP CIRCLING

When expanding the material, I re-evaluated my purpose, especially working on part three on exiting the roundabout. I have shared many times how I love my work and want to continue working, hopefully into my eighties. Just as many workers are now working remotely by choice, I have made the same opportunity for myself. The goals of more travel with my husband, additional giving to organizations, visiting our adult children, and expanding my circle of friends who are committed to an active lifestyle have pushed me to further schedule and automate areas of my business. With today's tools, this arrangement is entirely possible for a solopreneur.

I find immense satisfaction in helping and encouraging others to dig deeper to uncover their purpose in moving forward, especially if they've been circling, asking, "What's next?" My hope is that readers will be rewarded with a renewed purpose, bringing energy and productivity to their lives, calling upon their hero inside. I especially want to encourage those at mid-career or the halftime of life. Our world desperately needs the skills, resources, and experiences of those in middle age. I find many who discount their skills or have given up from fatigue, discouragement, or boredom. However, mid-life is the time when many have more freedom financially and can make career choices to pursue an area of renewed focus and passion.

The principles shared here are basic, yet powerful, and apply both personally and professionally. Most people do not experience just one roundabout in their lifetimes. Multiple roundabouts come with changes in the economy, relationships, a health crisis, and even projects. So even though the situations for each are different, the applications will be similar. While endpoints may vary, each person aspires to be happy, healthy, and content in her relationships, vocations, and the legacies she will leave. Individuals seek connection with others and meaningful work as part of actively living their best lives.

For those who are feeling stuck or in need of a little boost to propel them forward, I have created the three principles drawn from maneuvering and exiting my own roundabouts. I discuss the three "P's" of **Position, Perspective,** and **Purpose** as part of a journey of positive

INTRODUCTION

discovery with tools, suggestions, and stories to help readers assess their starting points, elevate their perspectives, and identify their purposes in life.

Let's begin.

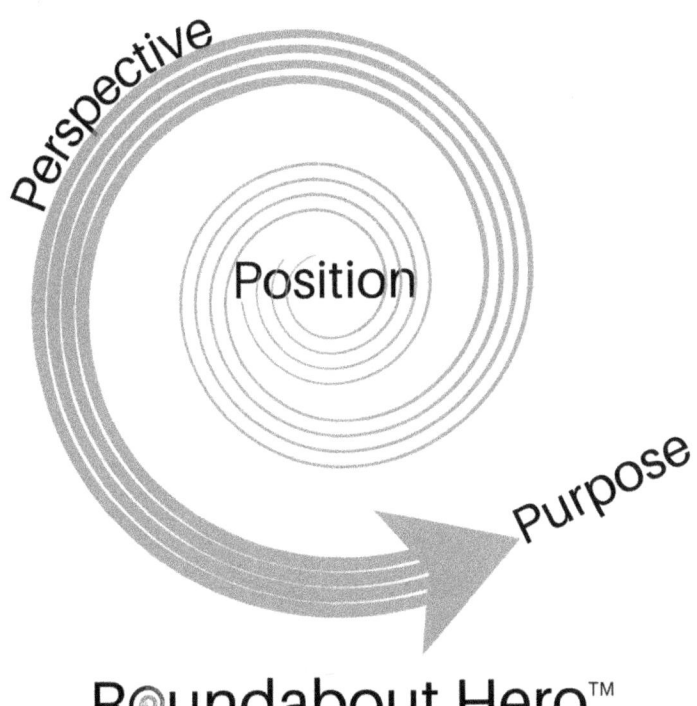

Roundabout Hero™

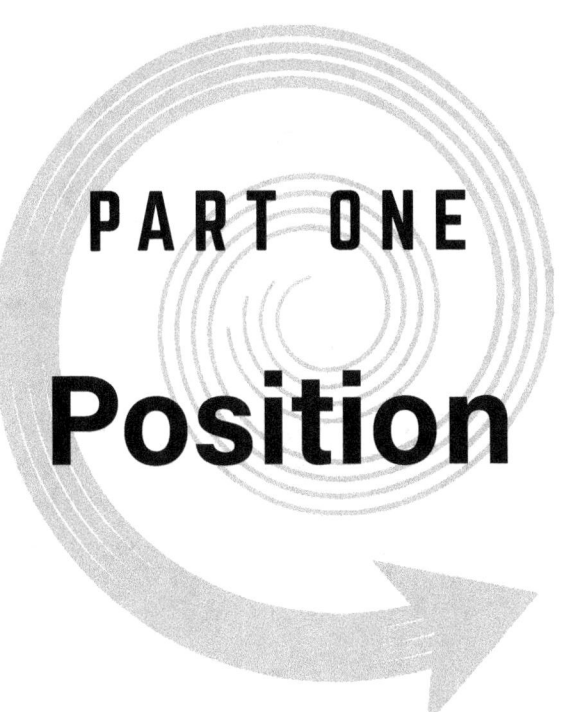

PART ONE
Position

Life's journey brings unexpected delights and disappointments. At times, our routes are clear, smooth, and obvious. Other times, our path is uncertain, muddy, and undefined. Sometimes, we move in a positive direction but then hit a plateau. Or we get stuck like a car caught in a roundabout, not knowing where or how to exit.

When one of our sons purchased his first truck, he was excited to see what it could do. After a period of rain, the back half-acre of our property that was mostly dirt had become thick mud. For our son, however, that mud was no problem for his vehicle! He had seen those commercials where powerful trucks would blast through any terrain. A muddy backyard? No big deal! Except it was. His shiny red truck zoomed forward, but without four-wheel drive, it hit that mud, sank, and stopped cold. The more he tried pulling forward or backward, the deeper the tires sank into gooey mire.

STOP CIRCLING

Like the wheels of that truck spinning endlessly in mud, we may find ourselves in frantic motion but going nowhere fast. Or perhaps our today looks no different from our yesterday so that we fall asleep at the wheel, awaking with a start only as we pull into our driveways. Fortunately, with a few tools, insights, and guidance, we can choose steps that can take us to our desired destinations. Defining our current positions accurately is a vital first step to creating a successful plan to navigate those confusing roundabouts.

We eventually were able to get the truck out of the mud. We located a sturdy mat and placed it strategically under one of the tires where it gripped. Then the truck lurched out of the hole. Similarly, when we learn to grasp this first step of Position, it could make a difference in our experiencing a successful exit out of life's quagmire.

CHAPTER ONE

The Roundabout

That feeling of fear that takes place when navigating a roundabout can also occur when handling life's changes and transitions.

A roundabout is often confused or used interchangeably with the term traffic circle. However, the road junctions are different. In the United States, traffic circles appeared first in Long Beach, California, with the Long Beach traffic circle[1] built in 1930 in anticipation of the Long Beach 1932 Olympics. With German engineer Werner Ruchti's design, the purpose was to ease movement of traffic among all the streets that converged at that area. He called it, "A multiple intersection without traffic lights."

Four main streets intersected in the middle with a large circle. From the outset, drivers felt fear about getting on and off the circle with its sharp turns and circling cars. It was ominous for most. In its first year, *The Press-Telegram*[2] called it a *death trap* referring to the four accidents on the interchange. Before the traffic circle was revised in 1993

STOP CIRCLING

to become a roundabout, my driver's training session at our local high school included navigating the dreaded circle. The prospect of not only entering but also exiting the circle safely brought apprehension to our whole class. I didn't look forward to that day of navigation and was relieved when it was over, as all of us exited safely.

Most of today's roundabouts are designed with clearer directions. The entrance and exit points have better signs and revamped merge-friendly lanes that are angled for safer entry. However, there is still some trepidation when drivers approach a roundabout, especially an unfamiliar one. That same fear can also occur when handling life's changes and transitions. Starting a new job or knowing when to exit safely holds its challenges. Further, some roundabouts in life have multiple exits. These confusing options can make one afraid to exit causing her to circle again and again, too afraid to make a change or take a different route.

The United States presently has nearly 8,000 roundabouts, a small number compared to the United Kingdom's approximately 25,000. In the same way, there are multiple roundabouts to navigate in one's lifetime and career. I have found most people understand the feeling of being stuck, circling on a roundabout; thus, it serves us well to consider principles for moving ahead in professional and personal areas.

CHAPTER TWO

The Assessment

*We need to identify where we are to create
the path to where we wish to go.*

Part of human experience is knowing how to navigate complex directions from one place to another. Most practically, this entails moving physically from Point A to Point B. As children, we learned to find our way to our elementary school classroom or our friend's home down the street.

As we matured, we employed our brains, time, and efforts to move between other A to B points. In school, teachers gave writing assignments at a time specified as Point A, and some days later, we submitted our work at a time specified for Point B. In between, we progressed through the steps of developing a topic, conducting research, creating an outline, writing the paper, and reviewing our work.

A—topic—research—outline—writing—reviewing—**B**

STOP CIRCLING

Similarly, as adults, we routinely create action plans to accomplish work duties. In managing projects, we pair tasks and timelines to move efficiently and effectively in order to reach goals and complete endeavors. This process has been crucial for me in creating music albums. Assessment of my Point A moves slightly after every recording session with a modified plan for the next session, but still working toward completion with a designated Point B in mind.

For most of our tasks, we are in motion, going from the start to the next step in completion of the project. For change or improvement, we first identify our present position, then create the path for reaching the next step. Developing life-change requires a plan. Thus, an assessment tool proves a valuable addition for our journey.

CHAPTER THREE

Halfers Tool

Exploring the different aspects of our lives can help us determine which facet may need urgent attention.

When I determined that my current career position was unfulfilling or unproductive, I changed course to make my life and work more rewarding. Now, I take stock of my work and my future goals regularly. I strongly encourage others to create the same routine. Conducting a thoughtful, honest, compassionate assessment of where we are today is a crucial part of reaching the path to our desired position, our professional summit. Periodic assessment is worth the time and the risk.

I have been a teacher in some capacity for most of my career. Consequently, I like providing techniques to aid memory, including mnemonic devices. Here is one that may prove helpful: In assessing my Point A, I use the **HALFERS Model** assessment tool. This framework represents the seven essential aspects of life that exert influence on how satisfied or unsatisfied we are. Further, they have impact on how successful we will be in achieving our personal goals. These **HALFERS Model** facets are *not* listed in order of importance. Individually, we decide how important each facet is to us.

Health · **A**ttitude · **L**earning · **F**inances ·
Employment · **R**elationships · **S**pirituality

So let's start by discussing how to determine our current position. Imagine that I ask a client, "How are things going in your life?"

After a quick assessment, the client may respond, "Pretty good, Deb."

That response indicates that overall, the person feels content. She is generally happy with life, though there are times when she may feel tired, down, or restless. With that general comment, this client has subconsciously scrolled through the facets and generated a quick, predictable conclusion. However, if some dilemma is weighing her down, she has to ascertain what that pain point is and then address it. Can she conclusively identify why her current situation is causing anxiety or pain?

In the same way, can we determine what aspects of life we would like to improve? Employing the **HALFERS Model** can help. Exploring these aspects of life can aid in determining the area(s) to which some additional attention may minimize or eliminate our anxiety or discontent. This model can help determine which facet needs urgent attention. Having been a professional musician and national recording artist, I visualize the **HALFERS Model** facets like faders—the volume controls—on a soundboard. A sound engineer takes the input of each singer and instrument, combines tracks, then shapes the overall sound by adjusting the faders, ever so slightly, to create exquisite music.

HALFERS TOOL

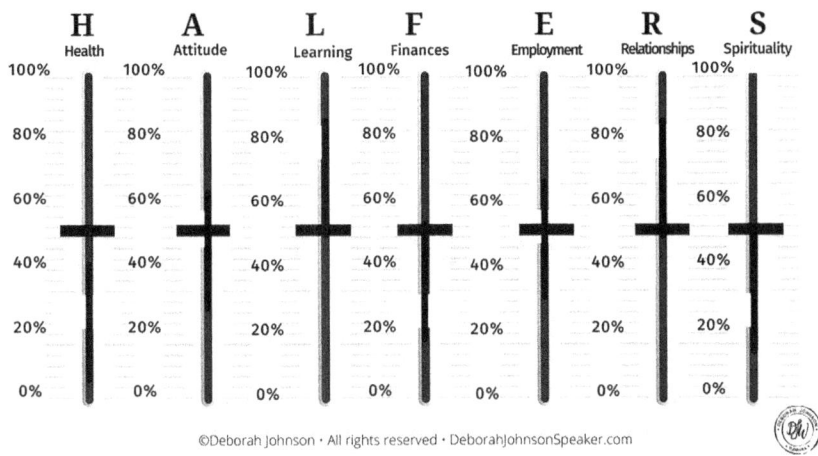

©Deborah Johnson · All rights reserved · DeborahJohnsonSpeaker.com

Similarly, as our own engineers, we can mix the seven essential facets of our lives. We create a blend of these seven inputs by turning one up or another one down. We each determine what is needed and what is best. We must be truthful, yet need not beat ourselves up with negativity. In the following chapters, we will learn how to evaluate and then develop a strategy, using each of the seven aspects. By establishing a solid position, we can pursue our own successful next chapter.

CHAPTER FOUR

How to Evaluate

When we are honest, we must commit to being equally forgiving of ourselves to avoid a paralyzing mindset.

Improving a life situation is not easy. We must address and act on matters or behaviors that we have previously avoided. Change requires full honesty about our past decisions, choices, and mistakes. Self evaluation compels us to accept that we are fallible, for no matter what image we wish present to the world, we remain human.

In determining our Point A, we examine each facet of our lives. After considering the soundboard with seven fader slides labeled **H**ealth, **A**ttitude, **L**earning, **F**inances, **E**mployment, **R**elationships and **S**pirituality, we can then ask, "For each facet, where am I now?" Once we honestly answer these questions, we can define the starting point for change and forward movement.

HOW TO EVALUATE

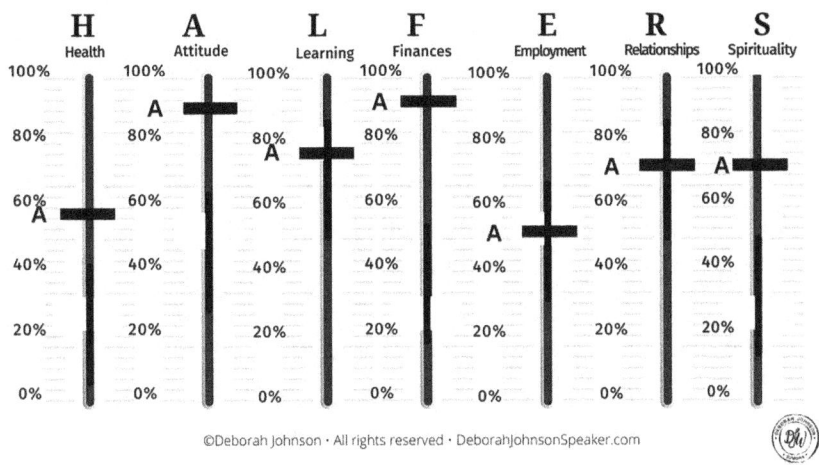

©Deborah Johnson · All rights reserved · DeborahJohnsonSpeaker.com

Being honest with ourselves can be discomforting and unpleasant. We have all committed errors that we may not be proud of. We bury the memory of events or actions because we feel regret and shame. Further, we worry about others judging us. We may have wasted precious time, either with unhelpful people or through wasted actions that created setbacks to achieving goals. This honesty includes taking responsibility for past actions and accepting their consequences. When we acknowledge those mistakes, we can let go of their weight. Thus, we reclaim the power that our past once held. We can create a more promising and optimistic future by acknowledging and accepting our missteps, forgiving ourselves, and establishing new plans.

    Furthermore, and this is vital, we must monitor the tone of our thoughts and weigh our words as we evaluate our current circumstances. We can be critical of ourselves in harmful and destructive ways. Or we can treat ourselves with understanding and compassion. When our inner voice criticizes, the criticism should be constructive not destructive. Inflating our flaws and mistakes only derails our ability to make positive changes. Deepening our appreciation for our talents, potential, and small victories moves us forward.

    During our self evaluation, we must be forgiving of ourselves in order to avoid a paralyzing mindset. The natural voice of humankind is to act as our own worst critic with negative self-talk. However, that should not keep us from conducting an honest and thorough evaluation of our current POSITION. It's an important first step on the journey to our summits.

My father owned a small, low-winged Piper airplane for years. He was always thorough in going through his pre-flight checklist. I remember impatiently standing by while he checked every item off. However, those checkpoints provided assurance that the flight would be safe. He also crafted a flight plan, even for short jaunts. Such plans in aviation identify the aircraft, equipment, departure location, estimated flight time and speed. This information is not only helpful in regulating air traffic but also in calculating fuel and necessary facts for any emergency assistance. Like a flight plan, we must know our current position, Point A, to navigate successfully to our intended destination, Point B. Determining our position may help us retain valuable resources for a smoother landing.

CHAPTER FIVE

Determining Current Position: Health, Attitude, Learning, and Finances

Evaluation of different aspects of our lives can impact our quality of life, our satisfaction, and our success.

This chapter focuses on the practical application of the **HALFERS Model** to determine the Point A position. The seven aspects of the **HALFERS Model**, impacting life quality, satisfaction, and success, are not listed in order of importance. That is for each of us to determine. After reviewing the definitions of health, attitude, learning, and finances, we can assess our current position. Later, in Chapter Twenty-five, we will find the full POSITION Assessment guide. It is important to take advantage of it!

HEALTH

Physical Health

*The physical body's functions and processes
support our physical and mental activity.*

Here, in examining physical health, we evaluate our bodies and minds regarding soundness, vigor, and freedom from disease or ailments. Here are some questions to ask:

- Am I getting the hydration and nutrients needed to fuel my mind and body?
- Am I making time for activities that improve my flexibility, strength, and endurance?
- Am I getting enough rest every day to allow my body and mind time to recover and reset?
- Am I caring for my mind, teeth, ears, eyes, and other parts of my body for long-term wellness?
- Am I engaging in risky or addictive behaviors that can put my health at risk?
- Is my health ready for the next phase of my life?

ATTITUDE

*A tendency or orientation, especially of the mind.
Attitude determines mindset in how we approach life.*

Many motivational speakers, from Edwin Louis Cole to Zig Ziglar to Stephen R. Covey, make the same statement: "Your attitude determines your altitude." I also want us to soar. Here, we will approach both constructive mindsets and mental health.

HEALTH, ATTITUDE, LEARNING, AND FINANCES

Constructive Mindsets

If we are willing to create a mental picture of what we want to achieve, here are some questions to ask ourselves:

- Am I changing my negative conversation by tuning out my inner critic and giving time to my inner advocate?
- Are the people in my inner circle positive-minded? Are they encouraging me to pursue my goals and to be my best self?
- Am I looking for (and finding) the silver linings in the challenges in my life experiences?
- Am I performing self-care activities that boost me, like listening to music or being in nature?
- Am I aware of and avoiding any negativity around me from social media or from complaining friends and co-workers?

Mental Health

Our emotional, psychological, and social well-being.

Here are some questions to ask:

- Am I allowing limiting beliefs to influence or block my progress? (This matter is especially relevant for entertainers, artists and professional athletes)
- Am I facing my fears or quitting with a sense of defeat?
- Am I identifying situations for which I am grateful, even when times are difficult?
- Am I seeking the help of a friend, counselor, or doctor when I am overwhelmed and in need of help?
- Am I getting enough rest from the demands in my life to stay positive and balanced?

LEARNING

The ongoing pursuit of new ideas, knowledge, skills, and experiences for personal and professional reasons. Lifelong learning helps us grow, even after traditional schooling is completed. It can benefit us professionally and socially and can even improve our cognitive health.

Here are some questions to ask:

- Am I scheduling a few minutes in my day to learn something new? (YouTube, podcast, etc.)
- Am I investing in my personal or professional development? (reading, listening to speakers, interacting with experts, etc.)
- Am I developing a new skill in an area of interest?

FINANCES

How we manage the money we have and earn to support what we wish to achieve.

Financial health has been proven to have a significant impact on our mental and physical health.[3] Here are some questions to ask:

- Am I living within my means by spending less than I earn?
- Am I on a path that will allow me to eliminate my consumer debt?
- Have I established an emergency fund to cover multiple months of living expenses in the case of a life-altering event? (job loss, injury, divorce, death, etc.)
- Do I have a plan to invest my savings for future needs including retirement?
- If partnered, can I discuss and collaborate on money decisions with my spouse or partner to create a financially stable future?

CHAPTER SIX

Determining Current Position: Employment, Relationships, and Spirituality

---

Pretense brings pressure when we are not being honest with ourselves or others.

This chapter covers the final three aspects of our current positions in life: employment, relationships and spirituality. Included here are a few questions to ask to assess our current position. (See also the Position Assessment guide, Chapter Twenty-Five.)

EMPLOYMENT

Employment is the engagement of our time toward a particular activity or person.

*It's our work, occupation, profession, or vocation.
Employment is not simply paid work for someone else.
It can include entrepreneurial work and volunteering.*

Here are some questions to ask:

- Do I find my current work enjoyable?
- Do I find my work meaningful or effective?
- Does my employment provide a good balance between work and personal time?
- Does my work satisfy my need to make an impact? Help others? (Again, employment can be entrepreneurial or as a volunteer.)
- Does my work integrate my skills, talents, and interests effectively?

RELATIONSHIPS

*How we are connected to other people.
The quality of the bonds we form has a
direct impact on the quality of our lives.*

Here are some questions to ask:

- Do the key people in my life share my values and support me in my goals?
- Are these people encouraging me to be my best self instead of holding me back or bringing me down?
- Do I have a person or group of people whom I can count on in times of difficulty?
- Do I trust that the people closest to me have my best interests in mind?
- Have I defined my relationship circles effectively to understand their impact on me?

EMPLOYMENT, RELATIONSHIPS, AND SPIRITUALITY

SPIRITUALITY

Holding a sense, feeling, or belief that there is something larger than ourselves that is a resource of additional power to live our lives.

Here are some questions to ask:

- Am I living life in a way that is aligned with my beliefs?
- Are my spiritual practices, including consistent time to reflect and meditate, helping me be the person whom I wish to be? To be a better person?
- Am I able to connect with a community of like-minded people through my spiritual practice?
- Is my spirituality helping me to be more loving, compassionate, and honest with myself and others?

Importance of Assessment

To start the Position Exercise using the **HALFERS Model**, please access the worksheets in Chapter Twenty-Five. It includes fader diagrams similar to the one below. The key difference is that the worksheets will not have the fader set to 50 percent. There will be no black horizontal lines on the worksheet so that we can annotate our fader level position, drawing in our own lines.

STOP CIRCLING

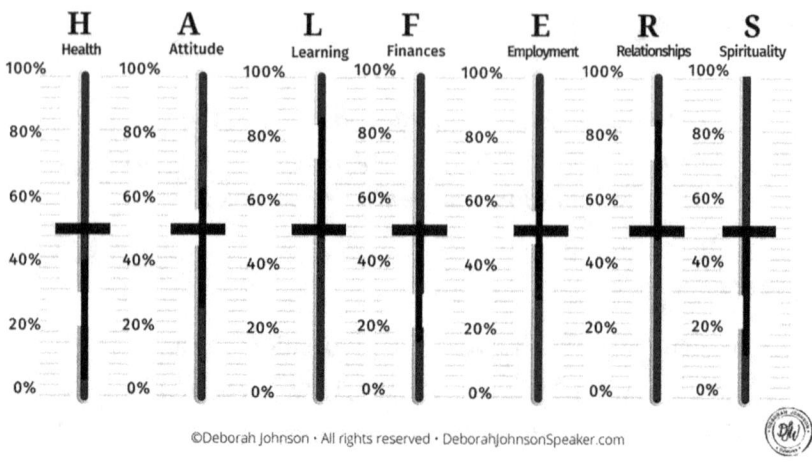

Using this diagram, first note the level at which we *currently assess ourselves* on Health, Attitude, Learning, Finances, Employment, Relationships, and Spirituality. Use the chapter questions as a guide. With the full exercise, there is space to record our thoughts. We can be brief or write additional pages.

Again, this exercise may not be easy. In fact, it may raise some negative emotions. In conjunction with this exercise, consider writing thoughts and conclusions in a journal. The process of releasing our experience to paper can be cathartic. It may also help to talk to a trusted friend or a professional if necessary. (Additional resources appear at the end of this book.)

Please stay with this process. It is worth the time to confront and evaluate each aspect as a critical step in the journey. My friend Susan's story demonstrates how powerful this process can be:

> Susan struggled for years financially. She had purchased several rental properties from 2002 to 2005 to build long-term wealth. When the real estate market crashed because of forces outside anyone's control in late 2008, she struggled to stay afloat financially. She couldn't sell her properties for the price she paid, and she faced substantial losses every month due to vacancies, increased taxes and utility costs, and a few problem tenants.

EMPLOYMENT, RELATIONSHIPS, AND SPIRITUALITY

After bearing her struggle alone for many months and punishing herself with distorted thoughts that she had made bad investments, Susan told her parents about her situation. Sharing her financial problems with family was difficult. She fought embarrassment and shame. However, she found that the act of acknowledging and owning her circumstances first to herself, then to her parents, released her from the heavy secret she was carrying and freed her to accurately measure her investment realities.

Susan felt energized. By being honest and accepting her current situation (her Point A), she was able to move forward to recovery. It took her several years to Improve her finances. While she resolved her problems on her own, she did not suffer alone.

This example demonstrates how *pretense brings pressure*, especially when we are not being honest with ourselves or with others. We can release stress and pressure by acknowledging our past with acceptance to create future plans based upon accurate information.

CHAPTER SEVEN

The First Steps

Today is the first day of our new journey.

Using the **HALFERS tool**, we can draw a horizontal fader line at the level where we believe we are today, starting with HEALTH, then progressing through the seven other essential aspects of life. This will establish our Point A. It may be helpful to annotate an "A" for each aspect.

To illustrate the process, here is more of Susan's story. In 2022, she repeated this **HALFERS** exercise to gain clarity on what she would like to do next. She was approaching 50, so while she was in good financial shape after selling most of her properties, she wanted to address the impact those financial struggles had upon her.

> Susan gained 30 pounds in one year when the stress of paying her mortgages consumed her with fear. Afterward, she was unable to lose the extra weight. Without significant change, her doctor warned that she was at risk for heart disease, diabetes, and possibly early dementia. Although

THE FIRST STEPS

Susan walked occasionally, she had rarely made her health a top priority.

She assessed her HEALTH at 55 percent. In terms of mental health, she felt great with the financial stress gone. However, In terms of physical health, she needed to take positive action to improve her long-term well being. She then completed her assessment across the other facets of the HALFERS Model, marking where she appraised her Point A (annotated as "A") for each aspect.

Overall, Susan felt her life was good. She had come a long way in the past few years. But where should Susan focus her efforts to actively improve her life?

The next steps in applying the **HALFERS Model** include determining Point B and developing an action plan to close the gap between our present position and our future goals. This step includes thinking about what our "best life" looks like for each of the seven facets. To apply this step, for each aspect on the HALFERS model, we add a horizontal line indicating where we want to be and label this fader line "B."

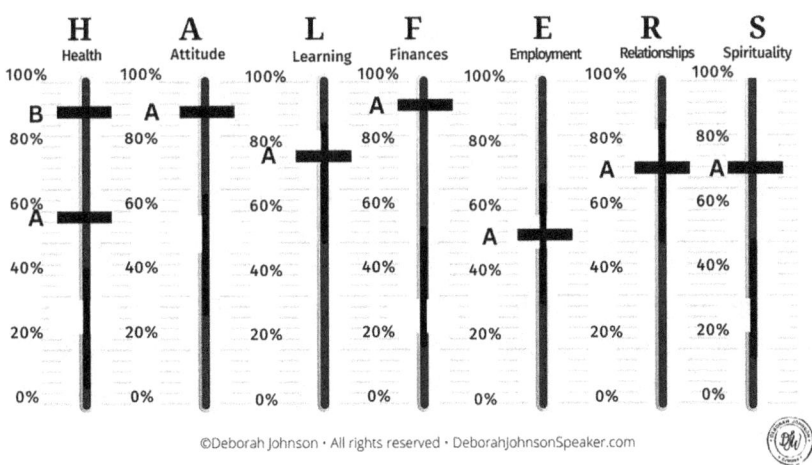

©Deborah Johnson · All rights reserved · DeborahJohnsonSpeaker.com

We could write in our Point B line at 100 percent for each of the seven aspects of our lives, but it is important to create a realistic balance between what is *aspirational* and what is *feasibly attainable*. Life is never perfect and striving for perfection is an easy way to become defeated before ever starting.

The goal is to become our best selves. Can we define what becoming "our best selves" means?

Consider how Susan assessed her Point B:

> *Susan wants to be more active, hike more, try a new sport with positive health and social benefits, like pickleball, and recover the athleticism and flexibility she enjoyed in her 30s and early 40s. She's not looking to compete in an Ironman Triathlon, though a 10K race (even if she walked part of it) would be an achievable goal. Commiting to a race would motivate her to jog and walk more frequently. Her current weight is 175 pounds, and her target is 145 pounds.*
>
> *Susan also wants to better understand why she gets so easily get derailed from eating healthy. She knows what she needs to eat to improve her health, but frequently she gives in to her cravings, then overeats.She assesses her Point B goal for HEALTH at 90 percent. She does not aspire to be a competitive athlete. Also she still wants to enjoy meals out (and a drink or two) with friends periodically. Her goals include improving her diet, her physical activity, and her flexibility. Susan, just like us, has to decide her next steps after identifying her current position and her optimal position.*

After determining our Point B for each facet, the next step is to compare our Point A to our Point B for each essential aspect. When we see the gap between our Point A (today) and Point B (desired future) for each aspect, do we feel positive or negative emotion(s)?

- **Positive:** We may feel positive emotions because we have, in recent times, moved closer to our goals. Or maybe, for a particular aspect, we have already reached our optimal point. We are happy with our current achievement.

THE FIRST STEPS

- **Negative**: We may feel negative emotions in seeing the distance between our Point A and Point B because we have not achieved what we (or others) think we *should*. Perhaps we are comparing ourselves to others.

Take a deep breath and know that we can change our situation.

- I am where I am.
- I can go where I want to go.
- I forgive myself for past decisions and mistakes.
- I can start again now.

Today is the first day of our new journey. Often, the first step is the most difficult.

CHAPTER EIGHT

The Next Steps

Acknowledging, owning up to, and putting our shortfalls in the past can start us on the path to making changes.

Sometimes we become caught in a holding pattern because we are unsure of our next step. Which exit do we want on the roundabout? How do we break this cycle to move forward? With the Position Exercise, we have established both Point A and Point B for each of the seven **HALFERS Model** aspects of our lives. We understand the direction in which we want to go for each facet of our lives.

What now? Here are five actions that can move us forward:

- Reflect
- Capture my Thoughts
- Brainstorm
- Ask for Help
- Act

THE NEXT STEPS

Reflect

Most of us are so busy "doing" that we rarely take the time for reflection, making time to slow down, be quiet, and think. Creating this space for contemplation can be challenging when we have demands placed on us by our families, our work, and other commitments. However, it is vital to find a time, a place, or an activity that is designated for reflection. One possibility is to establish a morning routine in which we start the coffee and then take 15 minutes for meditation. Or find a specific location where we go to think, such as a patio or a park. Another option could be taking a 20-minute walk after lunch for uninterrupted thought, which includes the bonus of improved physical and mental health.

My mother arose while the house was still dark. She retreated to her bathroom to reflect and pray in a quiet place. She needed quiet because my sisters and I practiced our musical instruments before school. Her bathroom provided space with fewer interruptions and less commotion. Currently, I take time early in the morning to read scripture and reflect, but not in the bathroom! I also exercise to start the day, which gives me additional time to reflect, away from the noise of a crowded gym.

Some fear this quietude and the awareness it brings, but for those who wish to be their best selves, it is important to tune in to our thoughts. They hold important messages that we need. After marking Point A and Point B faders for each of the seven essential aspects, we need time and space to evaluate our emotions and revelations. However, this contemplation period is not time to allow negativity or discouragement to occupy our minds. That behavior will keep us stuck, ever circling on the roundabout. Instead, we focus on positive thoughts to help us plan for the future. Reflection is a logical pairing with journaling. Once we have done some thinking, we need to do some writing.

Capture Thoughts

Journaling or jotting down notes can capture our thoughts, "empty" our heads, and prompt futher thinking. This download from brain to paper or phone, tablet, laptop or audio capture allows us to organize

STOP CIRCLING

our thoughts and plan the next steps. I have found immeasurable value in journaling to access and better understand what is truly inside my head and heart. By writing my thoughts, I reinforce my time of reflection and clarify my intentions.

> *While my husband does not call himself a journaler, he often puts his thoughts down as quick notes to himself. When an idea or inspiration hits him, he jots it down on a sticky note or yellow pad as his reminder to act or explore further. He did not grow up writing "Dear Diary" in a bound book, but he uses a method that works for him to accomplish the same result.*

We should feel free to capture our thoughts through whatever means works best. Journal entries need not be long or pretty. They simply need to be honest. When *we* maintain a routine practice of recording our thoughts, *we* can identify themes: What makes *us* happy? What makes *us* grateful? What steals *our* joy? Journaling is a tool of discovery, allowing *us* to dream a little or a lot.

If we're feeling stuck, we can ask questions like, "When do I feel stuck?" or "What are my future prospects?" If we challenge ourselves to write down responses to one or both of these questions every day for a week, we can identify our position. We are focusing directly on the challenge at hand, trying to stop circling the roundabout. The process of writing turns emotions (whether contentment, anxiety, joy, anger, awe, sorrow, etc.) into words that can clear our heads. Then we can visibly see our thoughts transferred to paper.

For me, my writing helps me move forward by setting new goals or exploring solutions to a problem. The health benefits of journaling[4] have been studied. They show that writing has a positive impact on mental well-being. I love writing with a pen and paper, so a notebook is my preferred way to journal. Others may prefer to type an electronic record for ease or for privacy. There are free online options, including penzu.com[5] (written journaling) and journify.co[6] (audio journaling), that allow anyone to encrypt journal entries. Also options exist for phones, tablets,

THE NEXT STEPS

laptops, and desktop. Some may like dictation, speaking thoughts on their phones. The benefits are universal.

Brainstorm

The question "Where do I want to be?" is not easy to answer. Instead, we can ask questions like the following ones:

- What activities fill me with positive energy?
- What would be different in my life if I reached my Point B for HEALTH?

(Note: We could do this for any or every aspect of the **HALFERS Model**.)

- What jobs would satisfy me while also allowing me to uplift and serve others?
- What does my ideal living space (work environment, spiritual practice, relationship communication, etc.) look like?
- What action can I take today to move me closer to a future goal?

Use this evaluation process to focus your thoughts on possibilities and opportunities.

Ask For Help

In my allegorical book *The Summit: Journey to Hero Mountain*[7] Mallery, the main character, was stuck in a town, job, and life that made her feel small, invisible, and deeply unsatisfied. To change her life, she struck out on a journey to Hero Mountain, overcoming challenge after challenge to find a more fulfilling, meaningful, and inspired existence. She overcame these challenges with the assistance of a guide.

We do not have to make changes on our own. Sometimes, we may feel like we have no one to help us. However, finding answers takes bigger thinking. Maybe hiring a coach or therapist is the answer. Finding a retired person from our fields to mentor us or seeking a member of the clergy or lay leader to help guide us is a possibility. Finding acquaintances with similar passions and forging relationships with them can help as well. One or more of these people can serve as an accountability partner or guide. There are also unlimited online support groups for various interests or issues. Some online courses are ideal for a deeper dive into a step-by-step process.

As we start planning our move from Point A to Point B, we can think about *who* can help us on the journey. Support from and partnership with others can be critical in helping us.

Act

In Part 2 of the Position Exercise Worksheet, which is in Chapter Twenty-Six, encouragement is to choose one act to do *today* that will move us closer from Point A to Point B. It's also helpful to write specific statements or commitments, detailing the three steps we will take in the next month to make progress. The most critical step is *taking a step*. Most journeys are never completed because they never get started. The exercise will help determine those first steps.

We will be asked to prioritize what area of our lives needs attention first. We can order this however we wish. Maybe one aspect of life is causing extreme pain. Or maybe another aspect has become urgent due to a health diagnosis or other life event. Or we could take the step that will be easiest to get a win under our belts and some wind in our sails.

The exercise will end with a commitment, taking actions in the next month to get us closer to our goals or desires. We can add these actions to our calendars with a process in place to hold ourselves accountable or maybe from someone who has committed to help us. Another option is to join a 30-day challenge or create our own challenge[8] to exit the roundabout and make forward progress.

THE NEXT STEPS

Summary

Conducting an honest and compassionate evaluation of our current POSITION in life is a critical first step on the journey to our summits and is necessary if we feel stuck. Using my **HALFERS Model** gives us more comprehension of where we are now (Point A) in each of the seven essential facets. Using this same model helps us define where we go next (Point B). Like a flight plan, knowing our current position is essential to getting to the desired endpoint.

Honestly assessing our situations—with forgiveness and compassion and without blame or shame—helps us determine how to make changes. Once we establish a direction, then we devise a viable plan to change. Reflecting, capturing our thoughts, brainstorming, asking for help, and taking action will allow us to execute a plan.

PART TWO
Perspective

We got the call while in the car. Authorities warned about an active shooter at a school in our son's city. At the time, his fiancé worked as a teacher in that school district. Our son had no further details, no indication which school was threatened. At that point, all we could do was pray for the safety of all the teachers and students. We also prayed that some hero would step forward to stop any violence. Within thirty minutes, officials canceled the school lock down. The threat proved to be a false alarm.

Our perspective during that tense half hour did not focus on personal problems, relationships, or agendas. Our primary attention centered on the safety of our loved ones. This incident examplifies how one's perspective can shift from the mundane to the truly important matters. These moments change our focus, thoughts, and priorities.

Being professionally stuck may not appear as crucial as this dramatic illustration of physical danger. However, if we are stuck like a

STOP CIRCLING

driver circling a roundabout and wondering where to exit, it can seem dramatic and endless. An alternate PERSPECTIVE can aid our next steps in making changes that provide an exit to the never-ending loop to nowhere.

PERSPECTIVE functions in three steps: to gain objectivity, to change a mindset, to picture change. So the first step is to use objectivity to gain a different perspective for our lives. We need objectivity to view our situation from an elevated point of view. The second is to define the mindset(s) that will enable us to pursue a change of direction. The third is to see our situations in a new light, to picture ourselves in a better, more desired vocation or position.

CHAPTER NINE

Perspective with Objectivity

To exit a roundabout, our lives may become more complicated before they become more manageable or rewarding.

At over 10,000 feet, Mount Baldy is the highest peak in the San Gabriel Mountains in Southern California. A fifteen-minute drive from our home lets us escape to a mountain village for lunch at the Mount Baldy Lodge.[9] Its cozy interior comes complete with a pool table and a full-antlered white tail deer head mounted on the wall. As we work our way farther up the mountain, we reach the ski lift that takes us to the peak. The view from Baldy's heights provides a vista far wider than what is seen at sea level. On a clear day, the vastness of the whole valley lies before us. Suddenly, we appear as just a speck on the mountain. We look small while the world looms large.

Just like those mountaintop views, a new perspective provides a broader view with numerous benefits. With a different point of view, individuals can assess their skills, experiences, and interests and open their minds to fresh possibilities. If one Imagines herself as a coach who would guide *her own self* from a broad, elevated standpoint, she may see opportunities not recognized before.Gaining perspective comes with challenges. Some may avoid considering any change because it is intimidating. To see one's life from the long view may also be painful. Yet the reassessment is worth the risk. Others may have reached a time in life when they have more freedom to change course, but they are unsure or unable to determine the next steps.

Other times, self-limiting beliefs cause a person to doubt his ability to make changes. Another inhibiter is fear from previous failed attempts to change. Then, there are the excuses: "It's just the way I am" or "There's nothing to see here!" It feels uncomfortable for individuals to acknowledge their negative traits, habits, or actions. Yet failure to address and transform these issues keeps a person stuck. Then regret sets in, and regret is like an annoying gnat, reminding someone of missed opportunities or of what could have been done differently.

Making progress requires a commensurate commitment of time, money, effort, and outside help. It takes significant adjustments to create a new way of life. When a person is true to himself, the change may impact others, sometimes negatively. However, it is necessary to let go of closely-held detrimental beliefs in order to accomplish new tasks or achieve new goals. Exiting a roundabout may make life more complicated before it becomes more manageable or rewarding. Yet the benefits of viewing life from an elevated perspective, seeing new routes and directions, provides fresh insights that are invaluable for growth.

How does a person gain the bigger picture? The following chapters on perspective with mindsets will provide proactive steps by using objectivity to gain an expanded viewpoint.

CHAPTER TEN

Perspective with Mindsets

How we think about our journey is a vital element in how successful we will be in reaching our summit.

To exit the endless circling of a roundabout, our attitude, whether positive or negative, is vital to how successful we will be in reaching our summit. An attitude is a mindset, and mindsets elevate and enhance our perspectives. What will our attitude be once we have viewed our situation from a wider perspective? If we don't like what we see, how do we turn our disappointment, regret, anger, or sadness into action? Here are several proactive mindsets that help us process the disappointments and obstacles we will inevitably face on our journeys.

Mindset 1: See Benefits Of Positive Change

Often change is good, but transition can be tough. When a woman is in labor, transition marks the baby's the last stage through the birth canal. That stage can be intense and painful. I can verify the pain of transition after having birthed three sons, the first weighing ten pounds! However, the reward of painful childbirth is great and enduring. In life and labor, the transition period is temporary, even though it doesn't feel temporary. In such times, it helps to focus on positive outcomes by starving negative thoughts that can cloud the joy of creating something new.

Mindset 2: Stay Positive Through Setbacks

It is unlikely that an initial plan will move someone steadily upward without experiencing a few setbacks. Setbacks make us scramble, feeling like we're picking up scattered shards of glass. Complications can include health problems, relationship conflicts, and work issues. However, we can boost resilience through belief in ourselves and our abilities. This resilience is enhanced by engaging supportive people in our inner circles, and through uplifting, inspirational stories, books, and videos.

Positive verbal responses like, "I can do it" or "I've got this!" will help us to respond instead of merely react. It's helpful to have notes of affirmation in various locations that are readily visible as positive reminders. Also, intentionally changing negative language to a positive reinforcement is crucial. For example, "I can't" becomes "I can as I..." Or "I won't" becomes "I will if I..." In theory, it sounds simple, yet the challenge comes in applying these mindsets.

Mindset 3: Compartmentalize Mistakes And Failures

Accurately acknowledging imperfection is not only necessary to define a person's current position, but also it maintains a healthy mindset since mistakes and failures are part of growth and change. With this evolving

PERSPECTIVE WITH MINDSETS

mindset, we put mistakes in their own category as valuable lessons and turn them into opportunities for improvement.

I've often told music students that song selections go to another level of expertise with memorization and performance, even if their performance is not perfect. Consequently, for many years, I provided performance opportunities for students, creating safe environments for them not only to perform but also to make mistakes. Afterward, we did not dwell on what went wrong but used the experience to learn and boost the students' resolve to improve. Likewise, when we reach the point where we don't want to risk making a mistake, then fear takes over. Fear hinders growth. We don't want to remain stuck in fear.

Mindset 4: View Roadblocks As Challenges

Just as tools like Siri reroute us when we encounter a roadblock, brainstorming alone or with trusted friends can help reroute our life's direction when we are deterred or discouraged. Additional help is available in inspiring videos and online stories. Further, we can request help from those who have experienced similar situations. Have the confidence to know that the roadblock can be overcome!

Up-and-coming surf star Bethany Hamilton[10] was thirteen when she lost her left arm to a 14-foot tiger shark. Afterward, she did not compete in the disabled category but continued in the National Scholastic Surfing Organization national championships. To compensate for her lost arm, she had to paddle twice as hard and to kick with her feet, but she remained competitive on a professional level, training hard and winning awards.

Mindset 5: Be Comfortable With Discomfortable

Leaving our comfort zone is often necessary when navigating the path to meaningful change. Doing so builds courage and confidence to reach accomplishments that we assumed were impossible.

After the years spent away from the spotlight raising our three sons, I worked with a coach, putting in many hours of repetition and work to create a one-woman headline music show. It was often uncomfortable and cost a great deal of my time, energy, and resources. I had to dig deep to find the boldness to overcome my discomfort with the commitment of making this role change and the difficulty of preparation. It would have been easier to stay where I was, but I knew in my heart I could accomplish more. As I fought through doubt, anxiety, and fear of failure, the perspective and clear picture of my success moved me to a successful result. These mindsets and stamina have proven valuable for negotiating additional roundabouts that have occurred in my life.

Mindset 6: Overcome Inertia

When we are stuck, either from fear or lack of effort, when we don't know where to start, or when we shun the risk of resisting tradition, it takes commitment to create positive change. The first step is always the hardest one like when someone recovers from surgery. For instance, individuals over age sixty commonly undergo knee or hip replacements surgeries. Fortunately, advances in technology are constantly offering better treatments for these life-changing procedures. Still, patients need some physical therapy. In fact, joint replacement patients get moving within twenty-four hours of surgery. Those first movements may be uncomfortable and even painful, but those exertions remain a necessary step in the healing process. No one wants any part of his body to atrophy with lack of use.

Similarly, making life changes may also be painful, especially if we have neglected some skills or training. Other people, accustomed to us meeting their needs before our own, may become upset or resist the changes we make. Some situations may get worse before they get better. However, we must take that step anyway.

Mindset 7: Erase Outside Noise

We will encounter detractors and distractions. However, we know ourselves better than anyone else, so we must stick to our convictions when pursuing a chosen path. We can push aside the negativity, dissatisfaction, or others' ridicule. Progress means we ignore the shiny objects and distractions that can capture our attention. This also includes negative self-talk. It takes intentional focus to move forward toward our goals.

> *My husband, Greg, was a relief pitcher for the Cleveland Guardians (previously the Cleveland Indians). Through the roar of the crowd, he maintained quiet in his mind when standing on the mound. He focused intently on his role—send the ball into an area about three standard pencils tall by two pencils wide, from sixty feet away at over 90 miles per hour—to beat the batter.*

A pitcher's mindset is a relevant illustration. For with focused intent, we can eliminate outside noise and direct ourselves towards our goals.

Mindset 8: Care For Ourselves First

Reaching Point B is easier when we take care of ourselves first. On an airline, when the flight attendant reviews the safety procedures, she does so for good reasons. Adult passengers are to put their oxygen masks on before helping others with theirs. If someone is incapacitated, she can help no one. In the same way, we should get rest through good quality sleep and stay hydrated. Getting to Point B takes time. Progress is not a sprint where we hold our breath until it's over. We can reward hard work with time for mental and physical relaxation and with fun activities. Even when fully focused on achieving goals, we must strike a balance to maintain our health and well-being.

For example, I'm most mentally alert when I take short breaks, by going for a walk, pruning a bush, or reading a book. These activities give

STOP CIRCLING

my brain time to ponder without intense concentration. Such diversions often bring unexpected solutions to mind. When we are at our best mentally and physically, we are more productive, creative, and better able to manage life even through setbacks.

CHAPTER ELEVEN

Perspective with a New Light

---

*By seeing ourselves in a new light,
we make accomplishing our goals possible, even probable.*

Most stage light designers focus on multiple angles when setting lights on a stage: front, side, high side, back and down lights. After they hang the lights, then comes the job of focusing them for a particular event. In small theatres, this process requires a technician to climb a tall ladder to focus each one. Every light and position illuminates a different element on the stage, bringing into focus a new view for the audience. Similarly, shining a light on ourselves to arrive successfully at Point B helps create a clear picture of our path forward.

By seeing ourselves in this new, illuminated light, we make accomplishing our goals possible, even probable. Professional athletes use this perspective to see themselves performing foundational skills with perfection; then they follow through with execution to win games and races. Entertainers use this perspective to see themselves on stage performing their lines and songs with excellence when preparing to deliver outstanding shows for their audiences. Creating this clear image of an intended outcome applies to both our personal and professional lives.

Let's again consider my friend Susan. (See Chapter Seven.) By acknowledging her financial mis-steps, she honestly assessed her current position and worked to solve some financial difficulties. With her financial house in order, she now wants to lose the 30 pounds gained from enduring great financial stress. Using this perspective, Susan can imagine herself as she was before the financial challenges—healthier and happier without the extra weight. Shining a light on an issue creates a clear picture of the physical condition she wishes to achieve at her Point B. She can use that image as motivation for a step-by-step action plan to become that slimmer version of herself. She might begin by prioritizing seven to eight hours of sleep nightly or, when stressed, spending 30 mintues outside for a quick walk instead of snacking.

Susan may combine her weight loss goals with other perspectives and mindsets. She can take an *elevated view* of her current situation and determine what advice a coach or other advisor would give her, as discussed in Chapter Nine. She can then apply the *mindset* of overcoming inertia to prioritize her health. Then, utilize the *mindset* of staying positive through setbacks to get back on her program after struggling to make healthy food choices, discussed in Chapter Ten. Combining these perspectives can be incredibly powerful in enabling anyone to move from Point A to Point B.

CHAPTER TWELVE

Perspective from Others

Rarely has any person achieved remarkable accomplishments without help from others.

While we celebrate "self-made" success stories in our society, rarely has any person achieved remarkable accomplishments without help. As we consider those who have impacted our lives, the list might include parents, other family members, teachers, bosses, co-workers, clergy, mentors, friends, and other influential individuals.

Marge Rivingston,[11] a vocal teacher, taught legends like Linda Ronstadt, Bette Midler, Meryl Streep and Sara Jessica Parker. When I worked with her, she first advised me to slow down as I stepped onto a stage. She said I was moving like a racehorse coming out of the starting gate, which resulted in a lack of connection with the audience. Her advice proved extremely valuable. As I took the time to slow down

STOP CIRCLING

and breathe deeply, I calmed myself before entering the stage. This change resulted in a more authentic and personable connection and enhanced my performance as I focused on the crowd before me. The habits I learned were not only helpful for performing headline music shows but for speaking at events and doing video work.

The perspectives others can provide—especially from those we trust—can help us progress to Point B. However, it is important to listen and follow through with applicable advice. Next, we will talk about how other perspectives can benefit our journeys, what we must be aware of when seeking the perspectives of others, and how to know if we have the right people to assist us. When we understand how we can apply the perspectives of others, we can determine which assistance is best suited for our situations.

CHAPTER THIRTEEN

Perspective from Input

A solid knowledge of core values will shine a light on ideas worth considering and trusting.

The assistance of others can help us achieve our goals in multiple ways. This chapter covers three Perspectives from Input. It takes discernment to determine what advice is worth considering and trusting. Before considering these perspectives, it is important is to first define and review our own *core values*. These are the absolute values we hold as priorities, as guiding principles. A solid knowledge of these values will shine a light on others' points of view. Our values can include personal commitments to family, spirituality, ethics, and even culture. (See Appendix 1 for an exercise to determine and review core values.)

Perspectives from Input

Input One: Content

Outside sources provide on-demand content through blogs, videos, podcasts, webinars, and other media. We gain perspective from the content creators without the need to interact directly. Applying what we learn from this content requires us to be self-starters, conducting follow-up on our own. We can use planners, journals, and other tools to stay on track. Many online courses offer on-demand content that we can access anywhere in the world. But according to online learning and teaching marketplace Udemy[12], the average student enrolled in a course completes only 30 percent of the content and an average of 70 percent never even start. So being a self-starter with a commitment to follow-through is important for accessing this perspective.

Input Two: Feedback

Others provide their feedback after hearing or seeing our career plans and proposed actions. While waiting for the chance to get feedback or periodic insights, different viewpoints, and suggested actions, we still have the opportunity to work alone. Sometimes feedback comes unexpectedly but brings immediate results. For example, we have a large set of iron candlesticks in our home with glass sconces that sit on top. For years, I complained that one of the candlesticks was defective as the glass did not sit evenly on top of the four small metal pads. I was considering hiring a welder to fix the uneven pad as I knew at some point the glass would likely fall, shattering into a million pieces. One night, we had a table full of company for dinner. One of our guests picked up one of the candlesticks and pointed out that both were standing upside-down. In all the years they sat on our table, this truth had never crossed my mind. By simply flipping both iron candlesticks over, their perfectly flat surfaces held the sconces firmly with no chance of breaking glass. Our guest's observation completely changed my outlook of our candlesticks. That incident remains a reminder of the value of good input.

PERSPECTIVE FROM INPUT

We can choose whether or not to incorporate outside perspective. I happily continued using our iron candlesticks. Now that they sit right side up, they provide a wonderful centerpiece for our table. For some situations, others may even provide action steps. We can absorb their feedback with the modifications that work best for us.

Input Three: Inspiration

Others serve as inspirational role models, especially ones who have already reached their goals and aspirations. Their stories of overcoming limiting attitudes and challenges provide us with lessons and wisdom that we can use for our journeys. For instance, an athlete like Lindsey Vonn, former American World Cup alpine ski racer, is inspirational. She continued to compete through multiple injuries until she retired in 2019. Though retiring was difficult emotionally, she listened to her body: "My body is screaming at me to stop and it's time for me to listen."[13] It was important for her to train hard, maximizing her abilities to compete at a level few attain, but it was equally important for her to end her career when she felt her body was broken beyond repair. We may never compete professionaly like Lindsay or achieve such a competitive athletic level, but we can learn from the life lessons she shares.

When someone else accomplishes a goal, we can see ourselves in them. Then, we gain motivation and confidence, knowing we are capable of similar achievements. We can learn from their steps and missteps. We may even consider asking them to serve as mentors or guides for our journeys. We also gain inspiration and perspective by reading biographies, books, and posts of inspiring individuals. Watching TED Talks or documentaries are valuable resources as professionals share their challenges, solutions, and results. Applying what we learn from their stories can help us picture and develop additional options to solve our challenges.

CHAPTER FOURTEEN

Perspective from Accountability

No matter what method, we need accountability to take specific actions and progress toward agreed-upon milestones.

This chapter explores three methods of accountability that provide valuable perspectives. They can be combined or used separately, bringing increased success and forward movement.

Accountability Perspectives

One: Accountability from a Program or Person

Outside experts can provide a program and materials structured to keep us on track. For example, we seek accountability when we hire a coach or trainer, sign up for synchronous courses, participate in a

30-day challenge, join Weight Watchers, or attend AA meetings. Further, we gain perspective from our coaches, trainers, teachers, and moderators, and also from others participating in the same programs. Within a structured system, we are held accountable to take specific actions and progress toward agreed-upon milestones. We must show up, report our progress, and even face consequences if we fail to meet goals.

Two: Combining Content and Accountability

We may need a combination of content-driven and accountability-driven programs to make progress toward our goals. This method works best for most as the combination delivers quicker results. For example, my friend Elise is a high achiever. Even so, Elise found that a content-driven approach was not enough to achieve success in particular areas. For example, she sought an accountability-driven program to help her downsize her belongings.

> *Elise read many articles about decluttering. She even listened to several episodes of The Minimalist podcast. However, she made progress only when she committed her money and time by hiring an organizational coach to work with her weekly. Although Elise is a competent adult, she needed the addition of an accountability-driven program to complete the decluttering she desired.*

Three: Input From Group Work

Others, like group members, can provide a structure of support to achieve our goals. Input from a team can be powerful, multiplying the effort and impact. Group members offer perspective, encouragement, and accountability. If we have an "off" day, they can cover for us and keep us on track.

Mastermind groups are a form of collective work in which the members support and guide each other, providing varied perspectives in

STOP CIRCLING

the form of advice and informal mentoring. If we have a challenge, a mastermind group can help us gain additional perspectives on how we might frame the issue, what resources we could utilize, and how to approach the next steps. Many professional associations have contacts and resources to find a mastermind group appropriate for various situations. With careful research, we can find not only professional assistance but also personal help with the right mix of contributors.

CHAPTER FIFTEEN

Others' Perspectives

Know that not everyone will understand what we are trying to achieve. Remember, this is our journey!

We can learn something from every person we meet. Nevertheless, we must carefully select whom we ask for specific feedback, advice, and mentoring, after first defining our core values. When seeking advice, discernment is crucial. Sometimes, we must take others' guidance with a grain of salt.

Sound and Unsound Advice

Every person's experiences are different, and not everyone will have the maturity and the breadth of exposure to provide sound, valuable feedback. Perhaps we ask a spouse for advice regarding a plan to obtain further training to attain a promotion at work. While our spouses may believe in the benefits of additional education, they might not encourage us to pursue classes because it could impact their time with us or increase their family and household responsibilities.

> Mallery, in my book, The Summit: Journey to Hero Mountain[14], sets out on a journey to find a more fulfilling future. Her brother follows and attempts to "save" her, as he believes she will fail. His actions are not driven by concern for Mallery's well-being. Instead, he seeks attention and validation as a hero and protector. Mallery sees through his pretense and continues her journey on her own.

Similarly, we must avoid seeking counsel from those who consistently demonstrate arrogance, rigidity, or pride. We may meet with their disapproval if we do not follow their guidance.

Perspectives on the Journey

When we commit to life changes, many will encourage and support us. We flourish with the positive perspectives of those who believe in our capability to succeed. However, others may not understand our need for adjustments and growth. We may even encounter some who actively wish to thwart our progress. It is important to clarify those who are *not* with us. Our goals are too important to be derailed by persons who are not fully committed to our success.

When considering others' perspectives, we should heed these guidelines:

- Understand the influence of a network on our ability to achieve goals. Associates can have an impact on our success.
- Use discernment in evaluating the motives of the people we consult. Do they want what we want?
- Ask, "Is this person still growing?" If yes, ask a follow-up question, "Is she growing in a similar direction as I am?" Situations are always

OTHERS' PERSPECTIVES

changing, and while long-term relationships can provide familiarity and shared memories, we may outgrow those who were previously important.
- Recognize biases in others' guidance.
- Have confidence to advance, even without the full support of close companions.

My friend Valerie is a mid-level military officer, and she has often sought the input of senior officers on what skills she needs and assignments she should take. If she talks to ten officers, she receives ten different opinions, often based on the path that led them to their high rank. She understands the value and limits of their advice. In the same way, not everyone will understand what we are trying to do. We can be forgiving and execute our plans anyway. When we show gratitude for the roles others have played in our lives, we can still move forward regardless. We are on our journeys, not theirs. Bringing new people and influences into our inner circles is helpful. We should trust our instincts and keep going.

CHAPTER SIXTEEN

Self-Perspective

Gaining self-perspective regarding our ability to achieve goals has immense power.

Most of us care a lot—maybe too much—about others' opinions. We worry if others like us, about fitting in, about wearing the right clothes, saying the right words, and doing the right things. Such worries are a waste of time and energy! We need to embrace ourselves, acknowledging our strengths and talents, to honor *our* perspectives. When we find validation, we can stop worrying about what others think and focus on what *we* think.

Limiting beliefs are the stories we tell ourselves, such as "I'm no good at relationships" or "I'm not creative enough" or "I don't have the courage to do this or be that." We repeat these stories to protect ourselves from rejection or failure. Perhaps others have criticized or dismissed us or our efforts. Then we internalized, accepted, and reinforced those perceptions. It is important to recognize and overcome such limiting beliefs that hold us back from achieving our goals.

SELF-PERSPECTIVE

To overcome such negative beliefs, we can challenge them. What made us think that we are no good at relationships or that we are not creative? By looking at these assumptions from another perspective, we can ask, "Are these assertions valid?" We can also ignore or change our negative inner dialogues. Most of us will not accept negativity or verbal abuse from another person, so we should not accept negativity from ourselves. When we pay attention to the words we tell ourselves, we can notice when we are unkind or unforgiving. Being aware of that internal conversation allows us to change the dialogue to positive, generous, and uplifting viewpoints.

Self-perspective regarding our ability to achieve goals has immense power. It can propel us forward to the destination we seek, Point B. We should not let negative perspectives derail us. The following principles are helpful when we falter:

Avoid Comparison

We can't compare our journeys to that of others. Instead we focus on our own journey. While others may be further along the path, their journeys are not ours.

- I am where I am.
- I have a plan and a goal.
- I am not behind or less than others.
- I am moving at my own pace.

Learn From Failure

We are not failures if events don't go as planned. Mistakes and failures provide invaluable lessons. To frame them as attempts, not as losses, changes our perspective. Even when a project does not work out as intended, we keep trying.

- What did I learn?
- How can I apply these lessons to move forward?

Start Any Time

What we can accomplish has nothing to do with age. Success is much more about will, persistence, and resilience than about a person's number of birthdays. It is about building upon prior experience, leaning into our talents, and having self confidence. Here are some inspiring examples:

- *Alan Rickman*, British actor born in 1946, reluctantly took on his first feature film playing antagonist Hans Gruber in the action thriller *Die Hard*[15]. He was 42. His critically acclaimed performance led to other villainous roles and characters with over fifty movies to his credit. They include playing *Severus Snape*[16] in the Harry Potter series, a role lasting over ten years with eight films.
- *Julia Child*, born in 1912 in Pasadena, California, grew up in a family with a cook, from whom she did not observe or learn cooking. Married at age 34, her husband introduced her to fine cuisine. She became so interested that in 1951 at age 39, she graduated from the famous *Cordon Bleu*[17] cooking school in Paris. After her contribution to the book *Mastering the Art of French Cooking*[18] in 1961 at age 49, an interview led to *The French Chef* to bring French cooking and her distinct voice to American homes in 1963, when she was 51. The show ran for ten years.
- *Ray Kroc*[19] was an American entrepreneur and mastermind behind McDonald's restaurant franchise expansion. In 1955, at age 53, he founded the McDonald's System as a franchising agent. Six years later, he bought the exclusive rights to the McDonald's name, and the rest is history with over 38,000 locations in over 100 countries.
- *Peggy Rowe*[20], American author with three *New York Times* best sellers, released her first book after age 80. She wrote every day of her adult life and persevered through constant rejection and a bout

with cancer. She's the mother of Mike Rowe, of *Dirty Jobs*[21] and is currently known as America's Grandmother.

Trust Personal Perspective

Others may declare that our goals are too lofty, unimaginable, or unreachable. However, if we can do it, then we listen to our internal voices. When we understand why others may discourage us, we can then focus on what *we* think and why. Our own sense of self, our abilities, and our desires should not be discounted. While another person may call herself an "expert," we know ourselves better than an "expert." Maybe a coach or mentor told us something that doesn't sit well. Contemplate and scrutinize the implication of those negative comments, journal if it helps, and even challenge those critical comments with constructive conversation if possible. Our opinions of what is best matter most. After evaluation, trust that opinion.

CHAPTER SEVENTEEN

Staying on Track

Our environment can support our goals or hinder them.

On a recent bike trip to the East Coast, our tour company provided a GPS app for our phones. It not only outlined each individual ride with a detailed red line but also voiced directions as we pedaled along. Our current location showed as a blue dot, similar to a Google or Apple map. As we pedaled in small groups, we knew if anyone separated from the group, he could still find his way and stay on track. This app instilled confidence and a healthy self-perspective in achieving the daily riding goals. We just needed to keep our phones charged enough for the app to continue running. Consequently, most of us carried extra chargers. For achieving personal and professional goals, here are additional suggestions to stay on track and keep our psyches charged for the journey to our personal summits:

Create an Optimal Environment

Our environment can support or hinder our goals. Living and working in clean, organized, well-lit, and inspiring environments provides a positive atmosphere. If we are not able to work in our optimal environment, then we can take breaks for the inspiration we need, such as being in nature, listening to music, dancing, or meditating. As encouragement, we can prominently display personal goals in our home and work spaces as reminders of our journey.

Format Goals As a Challenge

Challenges are time-specific accountability programs that encourage us to make steady progress toward a goal via incremental changes and growth. We can find many kinds of challenges online. These include the 4-week *Self.com*[22] fitness challenges, the *Whole30*[23] challenge for healthy eating, and the *Hard75*[24] for transformative mental toughness. These programs and others like them offer content like recipes and workouts as well as a community for support. We can also create our own challenge, adapting an existing program to support our specific goals.

Track Progress

First, we write goals for clarity, commitment, and accountability. Then we track our progress to build upon goal-setting by staying focused on execution. This accountability tool reveals our progress vs. our objective, showing whether we are on target or need to improve our game. Seeing tangible progress can boost motivation and momentum.

Employ Tools for Focus

The number of organizational tools, planners, and trackers is vast. Find what works best. Some may prefer an online tracker or a pen and paper pocket calendar. Some tools that have worked for me include the following:

- A daily planner. Planners allow me to time-block; I set times for tasks that bring me closer to my goals in my daily schedule. My current favorite is the *Planner Pad*[25].
- A bullet journal or other journaling tool. I clear my head by putting my thoughts on paper. I can then sort through my reflections to guide my actions. A simple spiral-bound tablet works too.
- A timer. A timer helps me focus. I set it for 10 minutes and get to work. Overcoming my inertia, I often get into a flow and go longer. This strategy is known as a "Pomodoro." Fun fact: The *Pomodoro Technique*[26] was invented by Francesco Cirillo. He invented the approach by marking 25-minute work intervals using a kitchen timer shaped like a tomato or "pomodoro" in Italian! I use timers most often for tasks I least enjoy. In no time, they're done!

Expect setbacks

Our perspective on these setbacks is what will help or hurt us in reaching our goals. The Stoics had a practice called premeditation. They would anticipate challenges by defining upfront what the worst-case scenario could be. They would then plan and be ready for this possibility. When we prepare for the worst, everything else seems more manageable.

Learn from mistakes

Like setbacks, mistakes happen. We cannot allow them to stop us. Instead, we can see mistakes as learning opportunities. Our perspective is vital to turning something negative into a positive. What did we learn? If we do a quick analysis or write a journal entry of the action we took and the results of our actions, then we can avoid repeating errors or making similar missteps in the future.

Keep a Steady Attitude

There will be days when progress feels too slow or we question if our effort is worthwhile. However, if what we are attempting were easy, we would have already done it. I find that journaling keeps my attitude balanced. If I'm feeling low, I read previous entries in my journal, gaining strength from times when I felt capable or happy with my progress. We need a plan to boost our spirits when the journey wears on us.

Keep Going

The best life is calling. It requires that we stay focused on what our future will hold and keep moving toward that possibility. What lies on the other side of the challenges will make the tough times worthwhile.

PART THREE
Purpose

In Bronnie Ware's book *The Five Top Regrets of the Dying*[27], read by over a million people in thirty-two languages, she pens the number one regret people have on their deathbed: "I wish I'd had the courage to live a life true to myself, not the life others expected of me." Sometimes others' expectations carry us through the whole first half of a life and even longer.

Defining a life true to ourselves is where the principle of purpose fits within the process of exiting an endless roundabout, making necessary changes. There is much talk about purpose today from a plethora of coaches and so-called *experts* who may or may not live up to the title. it is important to first define some of the basic fundamentals of purpose. Developing a purpose-driven life and business aligned with personal core values, especially at mid-career or the halftime of life, is the goal. Reading and applying the chapter instruction on core values in the appendix provides tools for success. It may be the most important exercise in this book since our values provide the basic groundwork for a well-defined purpose.

To be an expert in any field, we need to master the basics. This is why, even though I had studied piano for years and felt fairly proficient by the time I entered high school, my new instructor took me back to practicing basic scales and chords to teach me relaxation of the wrist, execution of fast scale passages, and to use arm leverage to play with strength and confidence. It felt strange going back to the basics as I knew my scales and chords, but her method carried me solidly through a professional music career. The wrist relaxation I learned has been an added plus as it applies to computer work as well as piano with no sign of carpal tunnel.

The principles of practice and repetition of the basics I learned have stayed with me in the reinvention process and expansion of my career. If the basics are solid for us, then the principles will also be transferrable to our fields of choice giving us the ability to build and expand. A solid purpose propels us forward. We won't need pushing. Now we can talk about purpose.

CHAPTER EIGHTEEN

Purpose vs. Mission

When we take the time to reflect upon our purpose, we make an invaluable investment in ourselves.

The word purpose is used frequently, especially in a self-help context. It is often used interchangeably with *mission,* yet there are distinctions between the two. A *mission* is the overlying arc of what one does—the business. A *purpose* is the unifying principle and answers the question, *Why?* There are over 5,000 results on Amazon for "books on purpose," a popular subject. One of my favorites is *Start with Why*[28] by Simon Sinek, where he asks and answers this question: "Why are some people and organizations more innovative, more influential and more profitable than others?" Sinek states that these successful people and companies all have something in common. They have first answered questions like, "Why a product? Why a service? Why a movement?"

Having a purpose is good, but what exactly is it? I found a useful definition in the article, "The Psychology of Purpose,"[29] from the John

STOP CIRCLING

Templeton Foundation website. This organization has a stated purpose of enabling people to create lives of purpose and meaning. They have defined purpose in psychological terms, such as "A stable and generalized **intention** to **accomplish** something that is at once **personally meaningful** and at the same time leads to **productive engagement** with some aspect of the world **beyond the self**."

Let's examine the terms within this definition:

- **Intention:** Choose actions deliberately.
- **Accomplish:** Set a goal and act to achieve it.
- **Personally meaningful:** Find significance in one's actions .
- **Productive engagement:** Complete actions for positive outcomes.
- **Beyond the self:** Impact others in a beneficial way.

While considering definitions of *mission* and *purpose*, the Walt Disney organization offers a useful example. A *mission* statement completes the statement, "We are in the business of..." A *purpose* statement goes deeper. The purpose, the *why*, does not change; instead, it inspires change.

Thus, Disney aims to inspire, to create a feeling. Their main purpose of *creating happiness for others* [30] flows through every aspect of their operations, from the ticket sellers to the ride guides to the hotel staff and to the entertainers.

It's a *happy place,* and as an entertainer for many years working with Disney, I have heard that phrase over and over from both kids and adults. Workers and managers have even painted inspirational phrases on the backstage walls. A well-stated *purpose* is an emotional aspiration. I have seen first-hand that people actually feel it in and around the Magic Kingdom. However, the danger arises when organizations, large or small, veer from their intended purpose, whether unintentionally or overtly. Blurred messaging causes confusion and divisiveness. Similarly, when we take time to reflect upon our purpose even if we aren't actively pursuing a business, we make an invaluable investment in ourselves. Then we can impact others by pursuing our purpose.

CHAPTER NINETEEN

Benefits of Purpose

Purpose is the engine behind the decisive exit of our roundabout.

For many years, we had a faucet in one section of our backyard that did not function. After re-doing much of our irrigation system, we learned why we were never able to get water out of the spout, no matter how hard we turned the handle. There was no attached pipe beneath the ground to bring water to the faucet. We could have turned the spigot as hard and often as we wanted, but still no water would flow because it lacked a water source.

Most of us, at some point, experience being stuck like a dried up water pipe. Being stuck can cause us to feel unsettled, anxious, depressed, or even despondent. Perhaps we are unsure of what to do when life brings changes, like being laid off, a shifting financial market, becoming an empty nester, retiring, or experiencing a change in health or marital status. In those times of uncertainty, we may find ourselves circling the roundabout, not knowing which exit to take because we are unsure of the route ahead. Doubt, confusion, and even fear may arise as we turn into unfamiliar territory. We are uncertain of the desired Position, our Point B.

Purpose is the engine behind the decisive exit of a roundabout. It is the source of free-flowing water for a faucet. Having a compelling purpose encapsulates what matters deeply to us. This purpose connects us with something greater than ourselves. Purpose has the ability to accomplish the following:

Propel Growth

When we are inspired, we want to learn, grow, and expand horizons. We want to know more, to fulfill our potential by performing to our best abilities. We expand our thinking, opening ourselves to new ideas and opportunities. We can fuel and solidify our purposes by becoming a sponge for knowledge by consuming quality materials and content, sharing and discussing ideas with others, and examining varied perspectives.

Focus Actions

When we feel stuck, we are uncertain which exit to take. A clear purpose provides us with the energy to narrow choices when choosing between multiple options. It guides our choices, illuminating the path we will follow. Despite living in a world full of distractions, we can enjoy greater focus.

Provide inspiration

When we are circling a roundabout, we can feel indecisive, lethargic, depressed—even hopeless. When we have purpose, we often feel determined, energized, and motivated to get out of bed in the morning.

Build Resilience

Life provides an abundance of challenges, great and small. Purpose helps us move through tough times because we know it is important to press ahead. Author Viktor Frankl, imprisoned by the Nazis for three years in four different concentration camps including Auschwitz, wrote the book *Man's Search for Meaning*[31] in 1946 after the war ended. He included a statement in his book attributed to philosopher Friedrich Nietzsche: "Those who have a 'why' to live, can bear with almost any 'how.'" Frankl's why—to be there for and to help others in the prison camp—helped him survive his own imprisonment. (See Chapter Twenty for a case study featuring Frankl.)

Create Deeper Connections

In our desire to advance our purpose and increase our impact, we may have opportunity to expand our network and connect more deeply with others who share our interests and passions. Purpose can also help identify those in our circle whom we may have outgrown. Each year, as I look through my goals and network, I identify shifts in levels of communication and involvement with others for the sake of time and energy. As time is our most valuable resource, I take this more seriously as I evaluate my future goals.

Draw In Others

Having purpose serves as a magnet, drawing in others who want to know more about our efforts and maybe even to join us. Our conviction and action can serve as inspiration. People may want to be part of our projects or use our example as a model to find and live their purposes.

Much of this interaction happens within trusted relationships, but developing trust takes time. Because cooperation and community are important, some of the 'hard-sell' promotional tools from the past are no longer as effective. For example, I decline promotions appearing in my inbox from social media contacts I barely know. I have had to block contacts who persisted in their relentless pitches.

Create satisfaction and happiness

We can chase happiness, but as Viktor Frankl explains, "Happiness cannot be pursued; it must ensue." When we focus on purpose, our capacity for happiness follows. Living our purpose can provide deep satisfaction in knowing that we are using our resources—skills, talents, experience, time, and money—to pursue something positive, impactful, and bigger than ourselves.

CHAPTER TWENTY

Why is Purpose Important for Us?

Our purpose can be different at various stages of life.

I have now shared what purpose can do—propel growth, focus actions, provide inspiration, build resilience, create better connections, draw in others, and create satisfaction and happiness. What do these benefits of purpose have in common?

- We are empowered to perform to our best ability.
- We connect with ourselves and others in a meaningful way.
- We receive immense physical and mental health benefits.

Purpose may also help us live longer. In *a study of 6,985 American adults*[32] aged 51 to 61 published by *The Journal of the American Medical Association (JAMA) Network* in May 2019, researchers found that a stronger purpose in life is linked with decreased mortality.

NPR covered the results of this study[33], reporting that study participants without a strong life purpose were more likely to die sooner, especially of cardiovascular disease, than those with strong purpose. The study results showed that the relationship between purpose and mortality remained consistent regardless of gender, race, education level, or economic status. NPR also noted that the association between purpose and mortality was so compelling that purpose "appeared to be more important for decreasing risk of death than drinking, smoking or exercising regularly."

A Case Study in Purpose—Viktor Frankl

Viktor Frankl (mentioned in Chapter Nineteen) was an Austrian psychiatrist, philosopher, neurologist, and author. He is the founder of *logotherapy,* a therapy to help people find meaning and purpose in their lives. Viktor survived years in Nazi concentration camps during World War II though his family perished. His book *Man's Search for Meaning*[34], written soon after his release from the Tuerkheim camp near Dachau, remains an enduring exploration of life, love, suffering, sacrifice, attitude, and choice amidst the backdrop of cruelty, starvation, sickness, and mass murder. Frankl found that, despite the dehumanization experienced by the prisoners, many held on to their sense of self. What did those who survived this unfathomable ordeal have in common?

While the survivors were not always the strongest physically, they had inner strength and mental resilience. Further, they had a reason to live. That purpose enabled them to stay strong in the face of abject misery. They needed to stay alive to achieve a goal: to aid fellow prisoners and retain hope of being reunited with their families. Part of Frankl's purpose in the camps was to help newly arriving prisoners overcome the shock of harsh prison life. He worked to keep them from committing suicide. He observed, "The more one forgets himself—by giving himself to a cause to serve or another person to love—the more human he is and the more he actualizes himself." Thus, the power of purpose is evident in the survival of many in those camps.

WHY IS PURPOSE IMPORTANT FOR US?

Some may be thinking, "Okay Deb, I got it. Having a purpose is beneficial. But how do I know my purpose?" Discovering one's purpose can be challenging. Individual purpose can be different at various stages of life. In the following chapter, I will discuss how to uncover one's purpose.

CHAPTER TWENTY-ONE

Discovering Our Purpose

We do not need to create something new to pursue our purpose.

When we were young, we were asked, "What do you want to be when you grow up?"

We received messages, explicit or implied, from others about what we should or should not become, what others wanted or expected from us, and what the "normal" or the "right" path entailed. Then we started on our paths. We applied for additional training and schooling, followed a talent in sports or arts, pursued an interest in business or science, joined the military, the Peace Corps, or a mission. We chose a place to live, or it chose us. We made commitments to other people, to spouses, partners, and children.

However, in the course of life, we may determine that some of those life paths no longer fit us or meet our needs. We may question our judgment, and even berate ourselves for poorly-considered decisions. It is possible to feel stuck in a situation because of past choices. While we cannot change the past, we can work toward new goals or career paths. That is a constructive perspective. Past decisions provide learning experiences and life lessons. So we can move forward with greater intention. In this process, many questions may arise:

- What if we don't know where to go?
- What if we are getting by and do not have the luxury of considering a new purpose?
- What if we do not feel particularly compelled by one strong purpose?

This chapter will explore ways to discover purpose.

Discovering Purpose

Everyone wants to use time and talents for valuable outcomes. Songs like *Ladies Who Lunch*[35] by Stephen Sondheim mock the well-off women who waste their lives at halftime doing nothing meaningful, planning brunches while they lounge. Writing about purpose always causes me to reflect on my life. I am fortunate. I want to work into my 80s, health permitting.

Through the years, the scope and direction of work may change, but staying active and influencing others in a positive way not only helps others but also helps us. I know people who feel compelled to optimize their time and skills, especially in the service of others. They are inspired by President John F. Kennedy's challenge, "For of those to whom much is given much is required." This statement was taken from the biblical verse Luke 12:48, written around A.D. 85. We have been called to be purposeful for centuries! In determining our personal directions, we should consider what purpose is and what purpose is not.

Purpose is Fluid

It can change depending on one's stage of life, interests, family needs, and work responsibilities. Sometimes, after pursuing a particular path, we did not find fulfillment or inspiration as we expected. This happens for many who obtain an educational degree but discover they do not like teaching and would rather do something or anything else. Good News! We can adjust and evolve our purpose.

Purpose is Practical

Purpose is more than the lofty mission of solving world hunger. It simply has to be important. Our purpose can be as foundational as bringing in enough income to house, feed, and clothe our families, which is critically important. Purpose need not create something new. It is not necessary to start a business, an organization or an event to find purpose.

Purpose is Multidimensional

We can join forces with others who have similar interests and objectives. Purpose need not be singularly focused. In fact, we may have more than one purpose. For example, we may be supporting family through work while also being the primary caregiver for our children or elderly family members. Keeping these thoughts in mind, let's explore a few ways to identify purpose. (The following questions are also included in Chapters Twenty-nine through Thirty-one, containing Purpose Journal Prompts with exercises for thinking about purpose.) Determining answers helps us discover insights into what energizes us. Then those insights move us closer to defining purpose.

Value Reflection

For me, finding my purpose took reflection. In thinking about which of my actions gave me the greatest satisfaction, I had an "a-ha" moment. I realized that I felt purpose in *what I was already doing* in multiple areas of my life, including encouraging others to be their best and to use their unique abilities and experience. I didn't need to find my purpose. I only had to understand that I was already living it!

For example, in my music career, I was helping others experience the joy of music, encouraging them to improve their skills. (see: *DJWorksMusic.com*[36]) In my family, I was raising three boys, encouraging and also disciplining them to be caring, competent, and contributing human beings. In my friend circle, I was bringing together small groups who could inspire each other and hold each other accountable. I was encouraging them to discuss, reflect, and commit to improving their lives. I've also led groups that prompt members to grow spiritually with accountability. These types of groups have also been incredibly beneficial to me.

In my writing and podcasting, I was creating content to inspire others, encouraging them to take positive action in applying their skills, experiences, and resources to become unstuck. (See *GoalsForYourLife.com/blogs*[37] and *WomenatHalftime.com*[38]). It was affirming to reflect on those areas of my life. I was already living out much of my purpose. I then felt more freedom to expand and refine each area with evaluation and reflection.

In the same way, others can evaluate their life directions. Many resources can us help find the best fit for future work or career direction. We can talk to those doing the kinds of work that interests us. Is their work appealling? Volunteer opportunities are abundant, allowing us to "test drive" different options without having to make a long-term commitment.

Difficulties of Finding Purpose

If we thought we knew what we wanted, but it didn't turn out to be "our thing" we should not be discouraged. Some need to go through trial-and-error to find what fits. Every time we try something new, we will get closer to discovering success. We can keep our perspective by viewing the time and effort we are investing as an opportunity to explore new skills and have new experiences. For additional help, read the chapters in part two on Perspective.

Difficulty of Transition

Change is challenging, especially when we have been doing the same job or working for the same organization for many years. (e.g. military, professional athletes, etc.) How do we know what we should do next when we haven't known anything else? It requires patience and an openness to explore new areas of interest. The questions provided above can help individuals test drive some opportunities. We don't want to put pressure on ourselves to determine exactly what we want to do for the rest of our lives. It doesn't have to be just one thing. If we don't like a choice we've made, we can try again.

Pursue Feedback

It's vital to have sounding boards for our ideas and future directions. A colleague or friend who is a cheerleader for our message or mission, or an accountability partner who can help bring our thoughts about purpose to life is invaluable. Verbalizing ideas helps us think through individual interests, talents, and options. Having an accountability partner, where we check in at determined intervals, prompts us to keep a steady course. Finding renewed purpose can be challenging, but the benefits can change a life!

The next two chapters discuss taking action, digging deeper into living out purpose.

CHAPTER TWENTY-TWO

Taking Action

The reasons and motivations for going deeper can be different, resulting in a different outcome.

Multiple scientific studies show that having a purpose benefits performance, relationships, health, and well-being. In Chapter Twenty, I shared NPR's summary of a study published by *The Journal of the American Medical Association (JAMA) Network.* In studying 6,895 American adults, aged 51 to 61, study participants without a strong life purpose, regardless of gender, race, education level, or economic status, were more likely to die sooner, especially of cardiovascular disease, than those with strong purpose.

In Japan, research into the impact of *ikigai*, a reason for being or a sense of life worth living, showed such notable effects on longevity that *ikigai* (similar to purpose) is now included in Japan's national health strategy. In a study of more than 43,391 Japanese men and women, not having *ikigai* was linked to *significantly higher rates of*

STOP CIRCLING

mortality,[39] including a 60 percent higher risk of death from cardiovascular disease.

When driven by purpose, we perform to our best ability, connect with others in meaningful ways, and receive immense physical and mental health benefits, even living longer and healthier lives.

So if we have been seeking our purpose, we have taken the following steps:

- Reflected
- Received others' perspective
- Journaled
- Talked with those with different interests
- Tested options to find a fit

After this process, we want to explore further. As we dig deeper toward our purpose, we need to recall *templeton.org's* definition of purpose: "a stable and generalized intention to accomplish something that is at once personally meaningful and at the same time leads to productive engagement with some aspect of the world beyond the self." When we go deeper toward our purpose, we likely already have a good idea of the purpose worth pursuing. However, the reasons and motivations for going deeper can be different. That may or may not affect the outcome of our next action plan as we ask, "What's next?"

In the next chapter on purpose, I will discuss how to define a stronger purpose and dig deeper to further clarify and pursue it.

CHAPTER TWENTY-THREE

Why Dig Deeper?

*Digging deeper does not necessarily mean work more.
Instead we can become more specialized
and targeted in the work that we have been doing.*

When working up a good sweat by trimming back bushes and trees in our yard, I remind myself how beneficial the cutting back process is for plants and fruit-bearing trees. In most cases, planting trees and shrubs will bring some fruit and flowers the following season, along with the weeds, of course. However, pruning and deadheading, trimming old growth, encourages new growth and usually more fruit. In the same way, it makes sense to dig deeper, to do some pruning in seeking purpose. Like a tree, purpose may be planted and rooted, but to nurture it to its full potential requires additional actions to encourage abundance. The following five reasons help answer and clarify the *why*.

Discover What Is Possible

If we have found satisfaction in pursuing our purpose, we may want to explore more options, focusing efforts on increasing impact. It is important to note that this step does not necessarily mean that we work more. We may instead become specialized and targeted in the work that we have been doing when digging deeper. This may take some extra research for that discovery.

> *For example, Holly started a freelance writing company as her second career. She loved to write and had enough clients to keep her working full-time, but she still needed and wanted to do more with her writing skills. After rethinking her workload, she explored what would bring her greater meaning and satisfaction. Consequently, she is now pursuing writing engagements on topics that matter most to her, including ocean conservation, coral restoration, seaweed farming, and other blue economy innovations. First, she did volunteer work with the Chesapeake Bay Foundation, writing about bay restoration efforts, especially oyster gardening. She also researched and contacted three non-profits that are re-growing coral ashore to then replant coral on reefs that have been bleached or killed by sustained high ocean temperatures and ocean acidity.*

Explore More Options

While we may not have found the best direction to pursue, may know what brings us meaning and satisfaction. For instance, an individual may have trained as a registered nurse. Her work in helping others gives her great satisfaction, but she feels restless. She has worked in the same hospital for several years. So she may decide to try something different and then commits to spending two weeks on an international medical mission.

WHY DIG DEEPER?

She researches various medical mission organizations. Then she decides on Nursing Beyond Borders, an organization that provides healthcare and education to orphans and poor children in Africa, Southeast Asia, Central America, and Oceania. Their focus is on disease prevention, so she will work with local health providers to offer free medical care to these children. She may spend two weeks working in the Philippines. While she may return exhausted, she is fully energized by the work. That experience motivates her to pursue future outreach. By researching nursing opportunities that impact people who do not have access to basic medical care, she makes plans to continue volunteering with Nursing Beyond Borders.[40] In the future, she may search for a full-time opportunity that meets similar goals.

Identify Issues Needing Solutions

The world holds many problems that need some intervention. There are heart-wrenching stories detailing how *400 million people in sub-Saharan Africa lack access*[41] to basic drinking water. A person who feels compelled to get involved may consider starting a non-profit organization to help with solutions for providing access to water in needy locations.

Solutions to these problems are not simple. For example, the *Water Integrity Network*[42] reports that much of the water infrastructure installed by other non-profits has not been maintained due to local corruption and mismanagement. This report shows that creating a new non-profit to provide resources won't solve the water issue. Government corruption needs to be handled first. So one approach to this corruption problem may include providing media tools and articles as an impactful avenue to tackle corruption instead of pouring money and resources into water solutions that will be squandered due to mismanagement, theft, and power struggles. The individual may start that non-profit but first may partner with an educational resource that can tackle the primary issue of corruption while he focuses on the cause that most motivates him, providing access to clean water.

Resist Boredom and Worry

When an individual feels her work is no longer challenging or rewarding, the situation may cause bordom or anxiety. For example, Linda worked for 35 years as a teacher. She felt her work was important, that it was her calling. She found great meaning in her teaching despite the demands of the administration and some parents. She gave her best every day to her "kids." Linda retired with a modest income that provided her with the freedom to do much of what she wanted. After several months of retirement, she realized that, while the freedom from routine and spending time with her children and grandchildren were wonderful, she felt less fulfilled than she did when she was teaching full-time. Consequently, she felt bored and a bit down.

> *To regain a sense of purpose, Linda volunteered a few hours each week to help adults with rudimentary language skills learn English. At first, she was hesitant to commit out of worry that she might miss out on other activities, but she found that the deep satisfaction she felt in helping adult students quieted that concern almost immediately. Linda knew that the time she invested in their learning would help them find decent work and better futures. Further, she still had more than enough time for the other activities she wanted to pursue in retirement.*

Seek Clarity

Maureen, an attorney, planned to retire at age 50. She asked her aunt, a Catholic nun, what she should do for her second act. Her aunt told

WHY DIG DEEPER?

her to "care for the poor." That is a wonderful purpose, yes, but also quite broad. While Maureen wanted to use her skills to help others, she needed to dig deeper, to uncover her reason and motivation for future outreach.

> *She volunteered with a few different non-profits for a period of months. During that time, she discovered an organization with a mission that she identified with most. She loved the work, committing to their mission to support and help protect women (and men) who had suffered domestic abuse. In reflecting on her decision, she realized her choice stemmed from abuse she had once experienced. Maureen's mission to help others who had also suffered abuse became a personal, meaningful purpose and a burning passion.*

These examples illustrate what is possible for those who want to make positive change not only in their own lives but also in the lives of others. Chapter Twenty-four will provide more information about how to discover new avenues of work and reward.

CHAPTER TWENTY-FOUR

How to Dig Deeper

---

*We all want meaning in our lives,
to feel that what we do matters, that we matter.*

After reading all the examples in Chapter Twenty-three, it may leave some of us wondering how those situations can apply to us or how we can dig deeper into our purpose. Below are some questions for personal application. They are also listed in the journal prompts in Chapters Twenty-nine to Thirty-one where we can take time to do the work and write our thoughts.

Complete a Purpose Statement

"I live to_____." "I love to _____."

It is important to explore what fits these statements for each of us. Being able to articulate what exactly gets us out of bed every morning is at the heart of defining and knowing one's purpose.

If it is difficult to complete either of these sentences with an answer that resonates fully, then we can try a different statement as a starting point: "I feel the greatest personal satisfaction when I am _____." Once the statement is completed, we can go deeper in clarifying who and what is most meaningful.

Create a Purpose Discovery Plan

To go deeper into our purpose, this plan outlines three facets to guide discovery: **Learn, Think, Act**. We can do some or all of these strategies. We should not discount an area completely as there may be a segment of great fulfillment to discover. The Purpose Discovery Plan outlines components of these three facets:

Learn: What to learn about and how to get the necessary information.

- Subjects: What topics we want to learn more about.
- Experts: Who possesses the knowledge we seek.
- Sources: Where we can find quality content to expand our knowledge.

Think: To explore and think through options for discovering purpose.

- Reflecting: What questions will guide our reflection.
- Journaling: How frequently and when to journal.
- Discussing: When to share our thoughts for useful feedback and guidance from trusted friends, counselors, coaches.

Act: How to experiment and test-drive options to develop purpose.

- Informational interviews: Talking with those who already work in our desired field.
- Volunteering: Offering services to organizations and causes that are of interest.
- Trial-Run Work: Spending limited durations (e.g. part-time, internships) to determine what work is meaningful and satisfying.

STOP CIRCLING

We all want meaning in our lives, to feel that what we do matters, that *we* matter. In defining a meaningful life, renowned psychological scientist Martin Seligman[43] states it is one in which we employ our highest strengths and talents to belong to and serve something larger than ourselves.

His definition sure sounds like purpose to me. I want us to live meaningful lives, especially during our next chapters of life. Facing mid-career or the halftime of life brings the stark reality that time is slipping away—fast. How we use our time, abilities, uniqueness, and resources can make a difference not only for others, but also for us. It is vital to create a discovery plan to successfully exit our roundabouts as a Roundabout Hero™. Completing these actions will fulfill in part *my* deeper purpose for writing this book: to help others create a simple, clear, and applicable system to make life changes by using their skills, experience, and resources most effectively.

PART FOUR

Exercises and Journal Prompts

To gain the most from all the information included in this book, it is important to take time to reflect and do the exercises included in the following chapters. Each section coincides with three main principles: **Position, Perspective**, and **Purpose**. Doing the work is the catalyst to move individuals forward in life, to successfully exit roundabouts as a Roundabout Hero™. Understandably, life changes will bring additional roundabouts in the months or years ahead, but the basic principles that a person applies here will apply to future challenges and will help individuals work through them.

CHAPTER TWENTY-FIVE

Position Exercise Part 1

The following exercise applies the **HALFERS** Model, which enables you to examine and assess the **seven essential aspects of your life**, shown like faders on a soundboard.

This exercise can take as little as 30 minutes, or you may want to spend longer to think and journal your thoughts simultaneously. You can be brief, jotting a few notes, or write additional pages. It's up to each person to decide.

In **Part 1,** you will assess each of the seven life facets individually, with current state (Point A), and the desired future state (Point B). You will also note what actions in the next 30 days can move you from here to there. For easier visualization, you can use a *different colored marker* for **A** and **B**.

I have provided definitions as well as journal prompts in this exercise as opportunities for reflection. Refer to Chapters Five and Six for specific additional questions to ask for each aspect.

POSITION EXERCISE PART 1

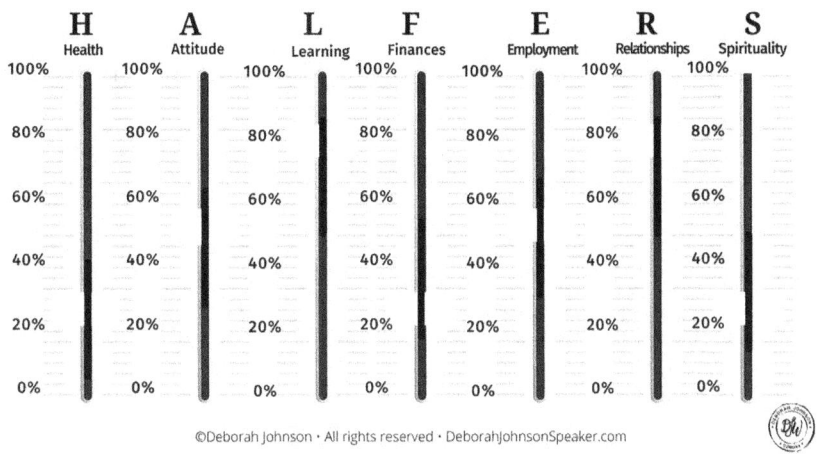

Health • Attitude • Learning • Finances • Employment • Relationships • Spirituality

Aspect 1 – Health Assessment Questions

Health: *The condition of one's body and mind regarding soundness, vigor, and freedom from disease or ailment. Can be influenced by mental and financial health.*

Step 1: ASSESS

On the **HEALTH fader**, mark a horizontal line at the level indicating your current position. Label this Point A.

Step 2: ASSESS

What considerations about your **HEALTH** influenced the placement indicating Point A?

The answers could relate to physical health, mental health, or life circumstances that are causing, either positive or negative impact.

Step 3: ASSESS

Mark a second horizontal line at the level you want to improve your **HEALTH**. Label this Point B.

Step 4: ASSESS

What does your optimal **HEALTH**, your Point B, look like?

Step 5: REFLECT / CAPTURE YOUR THOUGHTS

Compare your current position in relation to the steps required to improve your health.

When you see the gap between Point A (today) and Point B (desired future), what emotion(s) do you feel?

If you responded with a negative emotion, what is the opposite of this emotion? (Hint: This is what you can feel when you start to close your gap between Points A and B!)

Step 6: BRAINSTORM

What are three steps you can take in the NEXT 30 DAYS to improve your **HEALTH** to reach Point B?

1. _____

2. _____

3. _____

POSITION EXERCISE PART 1

Step 7: ASK FOR HELP

Name one to three people who can help you reach your goals for attaining **HEALTH** Point B. List how each may help you.

Step 8: ACT

What is one action you can take TODAY to start on your path to **HEALTH** Point B?

Aspect 2 – Attitude Assessment Questions

Attitude: *A tendency or orientation, especially of the mind. The mindset in how one approaches the aspects of life, including mental health.*

Step 1: ASSESS

On your **ATTITUDE fader**, mark a horizontal line at the level indicating your current position. Label this Point A.

Step 2: ASSESS

What considerations about your **ATTITUDE** influenced the placement of Point A?

Step 3: ASSESS

Mark a second horizontal line at the level you want for improvement of your **ATTITUDE**. Label this Point B.

Step 4: ASSESS

What does your optimal **ATTITUDE**, your Point B, look like?

Step 5: REFLECT / CAPTURE YOUR THOUGHTS

Compare your current situation in relation to the steps required to improve your **ATTITUDE**.

When you see the gap between Point A (today) and Point B (desired future), what emotion(s) do you feel?

If you responded with a negative emotion, what is the opposite of this emotion?

Step 6: BRAINSTORM

What are three steps you can take in the NEXT 30 DAYS to improve your **ATTITUDE** to reach Point B?

1. _____

2. _____

3. _____

Step 7: ASK FOR HELP

Name one to three people who can help you reach your goals for attaining **ATTITUDE** Point B. List how each may help you.

Step 8: ACT

What is one action you can take TODAY to start on your path to **ATTITUDE** Point B?

Aspect 3 – Learning Assessment Questions

Learning: *The ongoing pursuit of new ideas, knowledge, skills, and experiences for personal and professional reasons. Lifelong learning*

POSITION EXERCISE PART 1

helps one grow, even after traditional schooling is completed. It can benefit an individual professionally and socially, and can even improve cognitive health.

Step 1: ASSESS

On your **LEARNING fader**, mark a horizontal line at the level indicating your current position.
   Label this Point A.

Step 2: ASSESS

What considerations about your **LEARNING** influenced the placement of Point A?

Step 3: ASSESS

Mark a second horizontal line at the level you want for improvement in **LEARNING.** Label this Point B.

Step 4: ASSESS

What does your optimal **LEARNING**, your Point B, look like?

Step 5: REFLECT / CAPTURE YOUR THOUGHTS

Compare your current position in relation to the steps required to improve your **LEARNING**.
   When you see the gap between Point A (today) and Point B (desired future), what emotion(s) do you feel?
   If you responded with a negative emotion, what is the opposite of this emotion?

Step 6: BRAINSTORM

What are three steps you can take in the NEXT 30 DAYS to improve your **LEARNING** to reach Point B?

1. _____

2. _____

3. _____

Step 7: ASK FOR HELP

Name one to three people who can help you reach your goals for attaining **LEARNING** Point B. List how each may help you.

Step 8: ACT

What is one action you can take TODAY to start on your path to **LEARNING** Point B?

Aspect 4 – Finances Assessment Questions

Finances: *Managing the money one has and earning to support what one wishes to achieve.*

Step 1: ASSESS

On your **FINANCES fader**, mark a horizontal line indicating your current position. Label this Point A.

POSITION EXERCISE PART 1

Step 2: ASSESS

What considerations about your **FINANCES** influenced the placement of Point A?

Step 3: ASSESS

Mark a second horizontal line at the level you want for improvement of **FINANCES.** Label this
    Point B.

Step 4: ASSESS

What does your optimal **FINANCES**, your Point B, look like?

Step 5: REFLECT / CAPTURE YOUR THOUGHTS

Compare your current situation in relation to the steps required to improve your **FINANCES**.
    When you see the gap between Point A (today) and Point B (desired future), what emotion(s) do you feel?
    If you responded with a negative emotion, what is the opposite of this emotion?

Step 6: Brainstorm

What are three steps you can take in the NEXT 30 DAYS to improve your **FINANCES** to reach Point B?

1. _____

2. _____

3. _____

Step 7: ASK FOR HELP

Name one to three people who can help you reach your goals for attaining **FINANCES** Point B. List how each may help you.

Step 8: ACT

What is one action you can take TODAY to start you on your path to **FINANCES** Point B?

Aspect 5 – Employment Assessment Questions

Employment: *How one spends his time, including work, occupation, profession, vocation. Employment is not simply paid work for someone else; it can include entrepreneurial and volunteer work.*

Step 1: ASSESS

On your **EMPLOYMENT fader**, mark a horizontal line indicating your current position. Label this Point A.

Step 2: ASSESS

What considerations about your **EMPLOYMENT** influenced the placement of Point A ?

Step 3: ASSESS

Mark a second horizontal line at the level you want for improvement of **EMPLOYMENT.** Label this Point B.

Step 4: ASSESS

What does your optimal **EMPLOYMENT**, your Point B, look like?

POSITION EXERCISE PART 1

Step 5: REFLECT / CAPTURE YOUR THOUGHTS

Compare your current situation in relation to the steps required to improve your **EMPLOYMENT**. When you see the gap between Point A (today) and Point B (desired future), what emotion(s) do you feel?

If you responded with a negative emotion, what is the opposite of this emotion?

Step 6: BRAINSTORM

What are three steps you can take in the NEXT 30 DAYS to improve your **EMPLOYMENT** to reach Point B?

1. _____
2. _____
3. _____

Step 7: ASK FOR HELP

Name one to three people who can help you reach your goals for attaining **EMPLOYMENT** Point B. List how each may help you.

Step 8: ACT

What is one action you can take TODAY to start you on your path to **EMPLOYMENT** Point B?

Aspect 6 – Relationships Assessment Questions

Relationships: *How one is connected to other people. The quality of the bonds an individual forms has a direct impact on one's quality of life.*

STOP CIRCLING

Step 1: ASSESS

On your **RELATIONSHIPS fader**, mark a horizontal line indicating your current position. Label this Point A.

Step 2: ASSESS

What considerations about your **RELATIONSHIPS** influenced the placement of Point A?

Step 3: ASSESS

Mark a second horizontal line at the level you want for improvement of **RELATIONSHIPS**. Label this Point B.

Step 4: ASSESS

What does your optimal **RELATIONSHIPS**, your Point B, look like?

Step 5: REFLECT / CAPTURE YOUR THOUGHTS

Compare your current situation in relation to the steps required to improve your **RELATIONSHIPS**. When you see the gap between Point A (today) and Point B (desired future), what emotion(s) do you feel?

If you responded with a negative emotion, what is the opposite of this emotion?

Step 6: BRAINSTORM

What are three steps you can take in the NEXT 30 DAYS to improve your **RELATIONSHIPS** to reach Point B?

POSITION EXERCISE PART 1

1. _____

2. _____

3. _____

Step 7: ASK FOR HELP

Name one to three people who can help you reach your goals for attaining **RELATIONSHIPS** Point B. List how each may help you.

Step 8: ACT

What is one action you can take TODAY to start you on your path to **RELATIONSHIPS** Point B?

Aspect 7 – Spirituality Assessment Questions

Spirituality: *Holding a sense, feeling, or belief that there is something larger than ourselves that is a resource of additional power to live our lives.*

Step 1: ASSESS

On your **SPIRITUALITY fader**, mark a horizontal line indicating your current position. Label this Point A.

Step 2: ASSESS

What considerations about your **SPIRITUALITY** influenced the placement of Point A?

Step 3: ASSESS

Mark a second horizontal line at the level you want for the growth of your **SPIRITUALITY.** Label this Point B.

Step 4: ASSESS

What does your optimal **SPIRITUALITY**, your Point B, look like?

Step 5: REFLECT / CAPTURE YOUR THOUGHTS

Compare your current situation in relation to the steps required to improve your **SPIRITUALITY**.

When you see the gap between Point A (today) and Point B (desired future), what emotion(s) do you feel?

If you responded with a negative emotion, what is the opposite of this emotion?

Step 6: BRAINSTORM

What are three steps you can take in the NEXT 30 DAYS to improve your **SPIRITUALITY** to reach Point B?

1. _____

2. _____

3. _____

Step 7: ASK FOR HELP

Name one to three people who can help you reach your goals for **SPIRITUALITY** Point B. List how each may help you.

POSITION EXERCISE PART 1

Step 8: ACT

What is one action you can take TODAY to start you on your path to **SPIRITUALITY** Point B?

CHAPTER TWENTY-SIX

Position Exercise Part 2

In position exercise, **Part 2**, you will prioritize actions to take after you have assessed each of the seven aspects (or all that apply) in the previous chapter. This portion of the exercise will guide you through the order of our actions for the next 30 days to move us toward your summits.

Step 1: Reflect / Journal

Look across the seven essential aspects of life in the **HALFERS** Model. What do you observe when you review the marks for Point A and B? Is there a particular pattern or response that stands out?

POSITION EXERCISE PART 2

Step 2: Prioritize

Order the seven essential aspects of your life from the **HALFERS** Model by priority.

For examples, your number one facet could be the part of your life that is causing you the most pain, is the most urgent, or is the most important. It shows your highest priority.

Your number seven could be the part of your life in which you feel little or no action is required, is the least urgent, or is the least important. It is your lowest priority at this time.

Employment • Health • Attitude • Learning •
Finances • Relationships • Spirituality

#1 Priority: _____

#2 Priority: _____

#3 Priority: _____

#4 Priority: _____

#5 Priority: _____

#6 Priority: _____

#7 Priority: _____

Step 3: Plan

Write down your number one Priority **HALFERS** Model facet from Step 2 above.

STOP CIRCLING

Now refer to Position Exercise **Part 1**, Step 6 (BRAINSTORM) for the specific number one facet you wrote down above.

What are the three steps listed that you can do in the NEXT 30 DAYS to move closer to Point B in that facet?

1. _____

2. _____

3. _____

Using the guide below, create a plan and commit to it. In the NEXT 30 DAYS, accomplish these **three actions** to move toward Point B:

"On (x day), at (y time), I will do (action 1) at (location z)."

Action 1

Date: _____

Time: _____

Action: _____

Location: _____

Action 2

Date: _____

Time: _____

Action: _____

Location: _____

POSITION EXERCISE PART 2

Action 3

Date: _____

Time: _____

Action: _____

Location: _____

CHAPTER TWENTY-SEVEN

Perspective Exercise Part 1

The following journal prompts as well as other questions are meant to stimulate thought on how different perspectives can guide you to the life you seek. This exercise can take as little as a few minutes to jot a few lines. You may think and journal your thoughts simultaneously while re-reading the chapters to review. Be brief, jotting a few notes, or write additional pages.

Benefits Of An Elevated Perspective

Journal Prompts

1. Describe an aspect of your life in which you feel stuck. Take time to describe your feelings. This may be in a job or relationship that is not meeting your needs but you are too afraid to make a change. It also may entail hurting people you care for. Or perhaps you do not know where to start.

PERSPECTIVE EXERCISE PART 1

_____

_____

_____

2. Take an enhanced or elevated perspective of this aspect of your life. Imagine you are the coach hired to get you unstuck. As that coach looking on, sketch an objective picture of what you see. (Use stick figures or any object you desire.)

_____

_____

_____

3. What advice would you as that coach give yourself? This guidance can apply to a career change, relationship issue, health problem, or another aspect of life holding you back.

_____

_____

_____

4. Which mindset will you need to become unstuck in this aspect of your life? Can you describe how you will spark change? You can comment on any or all of the mindsets listed here or add your own. Refer to Chapter Ten for the full explanation of each.

STOP CIRCLING

Mindset 1: Focus on the benefits of creating positive change.

Mindset 2: Stay positive through setbacks.

Mindset 3: Compartmentalize mistakes and failures.

Mindset 4: View roadblocks as challenges

PERSPECTIVE EXERCISE PART 1

Mindset 5: Become comfortable with being uncomfortable.

Mindset 6: Overcome inertia.

Mindset 7: Erase the outside noise.

Mindset 8: Make self-care a priority.

STOP CIRCLING

5. In seeing yourself in a new light, imagine overcoming any obstacles. Describe and draw a clear picture of what you see and how you feel. (Use stick figures or any object you desire.)

_____

_____

_____

CHAPTER TWENTY-EIGHT

Perspective Exercise Part 2

Which Perspective Will Work Best?

1. Thinking about what is making you feel stuck, what perspectives from input (content, feedback, inspiration) and perspectives from accountability (accountability, combination content + accountability, group work) do you need become unstuck and to exit your roundabout? Refer to Chapters Thirteen and Fourteen if needed.

Perspective from **Content**:

_____

_____

_____

STOP CIRCLING

Perspective from **Feedback**:

___

Perspective from **Inspiration**:

___

Perspective from **Accountability**:

___

Perspective from **Content + Accountability**:

PERSPECTIVE EXERCISE PART 2

Perspective from **Group Work**:

_____

_____

_____

2. Who can help you get unstuck? (This could be a group of people.)

   a. _____

   b. _____

   c. _____

3. For each person/group you list in answering question 2, ask these questions about them.

   Does he/she/they have the ability to be open to the options I am exploring? Why or why not?

   a. _____

   b. _____

   c. _____

   Do they have a personal stake in my decision that causes them to push me in one direction?

   a. _____

   b. _____

   c. _____

STOP CIRCLING

Do they have my best interests at heart? Why do you feel a certain way?

a. _____

b. _____

c. _____

Will they be upset if you do not take their advice?

a. _____

b. _____

c. _____

4. Name the individuals, social/civic/spiritual groups, and professional clubs/associations providing you with learning, encouragement, and positive energy for your journey.

a. _____

b. _____

c. _____

5. What are some ways that you can foster and grow these relationships?

a. _____

b. _____

c. _____

PERSPECTIVE EXERCISE PART 2

6. Conversely, name those whom you may have outgrown or those holding you back. How can you minimize the impact these relationships have on your forward momentum?

a. _____

b. _____

c. _____

CHAPTER TWENTY-NINE

Perspective Exercise Part 3

The Value Of Self-Perspective

Journal Prompts

1. What limiting belief(s) do you have about yourself that may hold you back? For example, consider the following excuses: "I'm too old to do _____." " "I'm not creative enough to do _____" or "I don't have the courage to do _____ or be _____."

Limiting Belief #1:

_____

_____

_____

PERSPECTIVE EXERCISE PART 3

Limiting Belief #2:

2. What three points of evidence can you find to *challenge* or *disprove* this limiting belief? (Pretend you are an attorney making a case.)

Limiting Belief #1

a. _____

b. _____

c. _____

Limiting Belief #2

a. _____

b. _____

c. _____

3. Think about one goal you want to achieve. (If you've not defined a goal, then complete part two of the Position Exercise in Chapter Twenty-six)

a. How can you track your progress toward achieving this goal?

_____

_____

_____

STOP CIRCLING

b. What challenge(s) can you join or create to guide your progress?

_____

_____

_____

c. What tool(s) can help you stay focused on your goal? (See Chapter Seventeen.)

_____

_____

_____

4. Prepare yourself for setbacks and mistakes along the path to achieving your goal. What three actions can you take when you hit a roadblock or make a mistake?

a. _____

b. _____

c. _____

CHAPTER THIRTY

Purpose Exercise Part 1

These are journal prompts as well as other questions to stimulate thought on how defining purpose can guide you to a better life. This exercise can only take a few minutes to jot a few lines. Or maybe you will want to think and journal your thoughts simultaneously while reading the chapters on purpose to capture your thoughts. Be brief, jotting a few notes, or write additional pages.

Benefits Of A Purpose

Reviewing five important terms within their definition of purpose reveals the following concepts:

- **Intention:** You choose actions deliberately.
- **Accomplish:** You set a goal and act to achieve it.
- **Personally meaningful:** You find significance in one's actions .
- **Productive engagement:** You complete actions for positive outcomes.
- **Beyond the self:** You impact others in a beneficial way.

STOP CIRCLING

1. Complete the following sentence: My life feels most meaningful when I am doing_____.

   _____

   _____

   _____

2. Regarding the statement in question one above, describe why this action gives you meaning, significance, or satisfaction.

   _____

   _____

   _____

3. Think of a specific time when you felt deep meaning in your work or personal life. Describe that time in detail. What were you feeling?

   _____

   _____

   _____

PURPOSE EXERCISE PART 1

4. At times when you feel stuck, like in work, in key relationships, or in life in general, what emotions do you experience?

_____

_____

_____

5. Conversely, when you feel that your actions have purpose and meaning, how do you feel? What positive thoughts do you have about yourself? How do others respond to you?

_____

_____

_____

Note: These actions can occur during any time of life. Do not discount an action that may have occurred years ago.

CHAPTER THIRTY-ONE

Purpose Exercise Part 2

Discovering Your Purpose

1. If you were given a year "off" from life's demands to work or volunteer for an organization, which organization (or type of organization) would you choose?

    - What kind of work would you like to do for that organization?

    _____

    _____

    _____

PURPOSE EXERCISE PART 2

- What skills do you have that could apply to that work?

___

- What skills do you need to do that work?

___

- What problem would you like to help solve?

___

- Where would you like to work?

___

STOP CIRCLING

2. Why would you like to do this work or serve this particular cause? Does something from your life make this area especially important to you? Is there a reason you want to work in this area for future impact? (e.g. for your children, future generations, etc.)

_____

_____

_____

3. What skills do you have that you might teach to others? Who might benefit from learning the skills that you have? (This can be individuals or organizations.)

_____

_____

_____

4. If you were able to go back to age 18 or 22 or 30, how would you structure your life path differently? What kinds of work might you have pursued?

_____

_____

_____

5. Name three specific **causes** that you believe in. What excites you the most about the work others do and the impact they have in these fields?

PURPOSE EXERCISE PART 2

Here are categories from which you could gain clarity or inspiration:

Animals	Disease Prevention	Hunger
Children's Issues	Education & Literacy	Nutrition
Clean Water	Elderly Issues	Poverty
Conservation	Environment	Sustainability
Cultural Awareness	Health	Veterans' Issues
Disabilities	Homelessness	Women's Issues
Disaster Relief		

1. _____

2. _____

3. _____

6. If you could do anything you wanted for the next five years, what would it be?

_____

_____

_____

7. Did you give up a dream due to life circumstances?

_____

_____

_____

STOP CIRCLING

8. What was that dream? What would it take to pursue that dream or something similar now?

_____

_____

_____

9. After some consideration, write down three thoughts for each of the categories below:

_____

_____

_____

Type of organization I'd love to work with:

1. _____

2. _____

3. _____

Type of work I'd love to do:

1. _____

2. _____

3. _____

PURPOSE EXERCISE PART 2

Skills I need to develop to do this work:

1. _____

2. _____

3. _____

Locations where I'd love to work:

1. _____

2. _____

3. _____

Within your answers, you will find insights into what energizes and excites you. Moreover, in expressing these insights, you are closer to defining your purpose. Write additional ideas below after looking over your list of the type of organization, type of work, skills needed, and your ideal location. Sketch a picture of how that new focus would look.

Appendix

Core Values

When circumstances change, one's core values should be consistent and provide the stability that will aid an individual as he resets his course.

Maybe it's been a while since you've revisited your core values, or maybe you've never taken the time to define them in the first place. It is time to do this now. It will only cost a little time and some soul-searching to define and affirm the most important principles in your life. I have expanded this book with the chapter on core values here to help you in this process.

Defining core values provides a solid base for both your personal and professional life. They are the most important values because they reveal your driving force. They also provide the groundwork for a well-defined purpose. Additionally, this principled foundation fosters a character marked by consistency and authenticity. When circumstances change, your core values should be consistent and provide the stability to sustain you through difficult times as well as the good times. Review them often to keep them fresh in your mind.

In defining your core values, think of some words to describe your life, like *honesty, follow-through, fairness,* and *a strong work ethic*. These should be unmovable principles. In determining core values, you will focus on two central areas and expand on each: **faith** and **character**.

Area One: Faith

In what or in whom you put your faith establishes your essential source of truth. Whether it's God, science, government, nature, or yourself, this foundational core value creates a gravitational pull one cannot deny or escape. It is where you look to find wisdom in dealing with changing circumstances. Motivational author Zig Ziglar (1926-2012)[44] once said, "The height of your success is determined by the depth of your belief."

Faith beliefs and principles influence the way someone votes, one's medical decisions, giving, relationships, and close personal contacts. Most importantly, it's where one goes for wisdom. For example, *Hobby Lobby* owner David Green[45] credits his faith and higher power as the true source of his success. He chose to give his company to God because he believes God owns it anyway. Green's position may seem radical, but the timing of his decision makes his choice significant. Many individuals leave estates and large gifts to organizations after they pass from this world to the next. Green chose to give early to personally enjoy the fulfillment of his gifting. By doing so, he made headlines for his philanthropy.

Many put their faith in science and government during the year of shutdowns only to be confused with mixed messages from the media and government. This experience shows how important it is to put faith in what is constant and immovable, no matter what side of the aisle one is on politically. Barbara Dana (b.1940), American actress, producer, and writer of *A Voice of Her Own: Becoming Emily Dickerson*[46] states, "When public opinion takes a route far from one's inner conviction, one cannot value disobedience too highly."

APPENDIX

Some put their trust in themselves because they lack trust in leadership or even in a supposedly silent God. From the statement, "Everything is worthwhile except a strong opinion," many resort to listening to the many voices shouting their so-called truths, which results in confusion. To combat this, after you've measured your faith and the wisdom it offers, it's time to stop weighing all options and act upon the convictions your faith has inspired.

Area Two: Character

The attributes of your personal character are what others see the most. You can place these areas of character into building blocks to create a strong and solid foundational core. Growing up, I often played with Lincoln Logs[47], invented in 1916 by John Lloyd Wright, second son of the well-known architect Frank Lloyd Wright. I enjoyed playing with the wooden square-notched miniature logs, building all sorts of log cabins and forts, so much that, years later, I purchased a set for my sons. After the boys grew up and moved out, the boxes of old toys remained. Now, our granddaughters play with the Lincoln Logs. Consequently, I have added to the supply, encouraging them to use their imaginations in building larger buildings.

Lincoln Logs cannot stand without a flat, solid base because firm foundations are most important in any building project. In the same way, identifying strong foundational principles while building, level upon level, is necessary to define a strong character. Imagine a design in the shape of a pyramid with multiple levels. At the foundational level lies the most essential character quality. Take a moment to define how each of these character qualities applies to you and determine what is most important in your personal and professional life.

Building Layers of Character

Layer One, Respect

This includes respecting others as well as yourself. A general lack of respect is evident today, expressed in protests, anger, divorce, and war. It is even visible in individual personal habits and images. Take a hard look in the mirror. Do you respect yourself enough to care about your personal image and health? Take a moment to define how you communicate respect to others and to yourself. Do you live a life worthy of respect or instead, do you demand respect? Is the quality of your work worthy of respect?

Layer Two, Trust

With our world of so-called *experts,* who is worthy of your trust? Are you trustworthy? Once a brand loses trust, the company usually loses business unless that trust can be regained. When Tylenol capsules were found laced with cyanide in October 1982[48], the manufacturer, Johnson & Johnson, immediately recalled the more than 31 million bottles of Tylenol in circulation. They also took an active role with the media in issuing mass warnings. They immediately put new product protection methods in place. This is why many products are now factory sealed. Through honest, effective efforts, Johnson & Johnson regained consumers' trust. However, mandatory factory seals have brought challenges because opening some of those products is nearly impossible!

How are you building trust? Trust can be developed or regained with good communication, meaningful content, research, and consistency. Most entrepreneurs and businesses create volumes of good quality content that is well-sourced and applicable because those efforts develop trust for consumer and business prospects.

Layer Three, Dependability

According to the *American Pet Products Association (APPA)*[49], 70 percent of households owned a pet in 2021-2022. When I think of our dog

APPENDIX

Amelia, I think of dependability. She always greets me by running in circles and with a wagging tail. Dependability builds trust because contacts, customers, and even family members know they can rely on you. How dependable are you? How are you demonstrating that dependability?

Layer Four, Thoroughness

Many creative souls tend to jump from one project to another since they develop enough ideas to fill a stadium. I have been guilty of jumping from project to project. However, I have learned to focus and finish projects with well-defined tasks. Some people have a special knack and passion for thoroughness, so high-energy creatives do well to surround themselves with trusted contacts possessing this trait. For me personally, paying attention to important details has helped me to create priorities that lead me to completion of my projects. The danger lies in getting caught up in minor details where we can easily lose sight of the big picture or the real goals.

Layer Five, Initiative

Not everyone is an initiator, but almost everyone can develop initiative—the ability to see a need and then to fulfill it. I love it when my husband takes the initiative to finish dishes or vacuum, especially when I'm in the middle of a writing project. It's what a team member can do by finishing certain tasks so leaders can do their jobs more effectively. Conversely, leaders can give specific instructions to help their team members progress more quickly.

Layer Six, Creativity

Does anybody think for themselves anymore? Problems develop when individuals lack critical thinking skills. Often people follow the crowd like sheep, blinded by *group think*. A classic example comes from the

2015 report out of Istanbul, Turkey, where one sheep jumped to its death, and 1,500 other sheep followed.[50] Likewise, many writers follow the *group think* pattern. How many books have you read that merely repeat the same message, just in a slightly different way? Bookstores display this problem front and center with shelves filled with books all purporting the same ideas, authors merely following the crowd. Although creativity doesn't mean you have to be an independent artist, songwriter, or author, it does entail thinking for yourself, finding truth, and being original.

Organizations that follow the latest so-called *relevant messaging* often lose their way. Consequently, they drift far from their founding mission. For a moment, these companies or foundations see themselves representing cutting-edge interests relevant to the whole of society, but most times, these movements create a divided organization that loses effectiveness and overall influence.

I know of arts organizations, churches and other non-profits that have abandoned their missions in search of "cultural relevance" and found themselves in serious predicaments and difficult circumstances. Even Elizabeth Gaskell (1810-1865)[51], a popular nineteenth-century author stated that what others thought as right or wrong was nothing compared to her own innate conviction and knowledge of what was morally wrong. Thus, she was not swayed by other's opinions but by her unwavering moral code. Whether writing in the 1800s or in the present day, using creativity is to be bold enough to do something uncommon.

How will Others See You?

When others look at your life, do they see a person of integrity and faith? Or do they see a grumpy old person? When thinking through your values, realize that having strong values will positively influence those around you. If you are focusing mainly on creating wealth, the pressure of obtaining that wealth may make you an unpleasant person. Individuals are generally a reflection of what they read, what they watch,

APPENDIX

and of the five people with whom they spend the most time.

Many think more about their purpose and core values when entering the second half of life, especially if they have worked hard at building a career and a business and are ready for a change. They realize that now is the time to create more significance and make the world a better place for the next generation because later may come sooner than they imagine.

Those with solid core values find tremendous peace of mind. Learning to be honest, generous, respectful, trustworthy, and kind can be more effective than many therapy sessions. Spend time now thinking through or re-evaluating your core values.

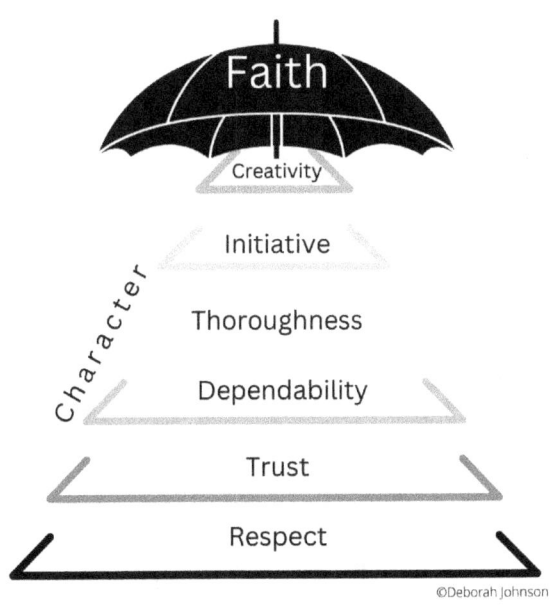

Application: Your Life's Foundational Principles

First, define the words or phrases that speak of your values in two main areas. Then compose three short statements or principles that reflect your core values and beliefs. This process is for you and need not be eloquent, only honest. The statements can center on integrity, faith, or mission. They may even include the type of legacy you want to leave. Going through this process will help you in determining your next steps, no matter your stage of life. You can add more principles, but keep it simple, preferably five or less.

Faith

_____

_____

_____

Character

- Respect
- Trust
- Dependability
- Thoroughness
- Initiative
- Creativity

Principle One that reflects my core values and beliefs:

_____

_____

_____

APPENDIX

Principle Two that reflects my core values and beliefs:

_____

_____

_____

Principle Three that reflects my core values and beliefs:

_____

_____

_____

About the Author

Deborah Johnson, M.A., is an author, speaker, composer, and performer. *Stop Circling* is her sixth book but certainly not her first major project. She has released multiple albums as well as written hundreds of songs and three full-length musicals. In addition, she produces a popular podcast *Women at Halftime,* focusing on mid-career transitions and the halftime of life.

Deborah loves to create and is energized by the creative process. A teacher at heart, she is especially moved when others learn and move beyond their fears and self-limiting beliefs after accessing one of her products. Along with writing and creating, she loves the outdoors and plans active getaways with her husband, a former professional athlete, to keep them both in shape. Her children and grandchildren hold a special place in her heart and will always be one of her life's priorities.

While being up for multiple **GRAMMY Awards**® and spending over 20 years in the entertainment industry, **Deborah** has also built multiple self-driven businesses. She speaks and performs in both live and virtual events, using her uniqueness and skills to help others exit their roundabouts successfully to climb their personal summits.

RESOURCES

I always encourage those who need professional help to get it. My online courses and resources will help you grow personally and professionally, but if you need additional financial or emotional counseling, don't put it off. However, don't continue circling in the counseling space longer than needed. Do the work and have the courage and strength to move forward.

Many of my resources are listed here:

Online Courses: *https://GoalsForYourLife.com/online-learning/*

Books and Products: *https://goalsforyourlife.com/goal-setting-products/*

Sheet Music: *https://djworksmusic.com/sheet-music/*

Musicals: *https://djworksmusic.com/musicals/*

Music Albums & Products: *https://djworksmusic.com/products/*

Free Downloads: *https://GoalsForYourLife.com/DJWorks/*

Speaking Topics: *https://DeborahJohnsonSpeaker.com*

PURPOSE EXERCISE PART 2

STOP CIRCLING

ENDNOTES

1. D.J. Waldie, "Spinning Wheel Turns," *KCET SoCal Focus blog*, September 19, 2011, https://www.kcet.org/socal-focus/spinning-wheel-turns#:~:text=So%20the%20Long%20Beach%20circle,was%20German%20engineer%20Werner%20Ruchti.

2. Tim Grobaty, "The Traffic Circle's Roundabout History," *Press-Telegram e-Edition*, updated September 1, 2017, https://www.presstelegram.com/2011/09/12/tim-grobaty-the-traffic-circles-roundabout-history/

3. Elizabeth Scott, PhD, "Financial Stress: How to Cope," *VeryWell Mind*, updatd July 29, 2022, https://www.verywellmind.com/understanding-and-preventing-financial-stress-3144546

4. Margarita Tartakovsky, "6 Journaling Benefits and How to Start Right Now," *Healthline blog*, updated February 22, 2022, https://www.healthline.com/health/benefits-of-journaling%23self-discovery

5. https://penzu.com/

6. https://journify.co/

7. Deborah Johnson, *The Summit: Journey to Hero Mountain*, (2021), https://www.amazon.com/Summit-Journey-Hero-Mountain/dp/1733348417

8. John Turner, "How to Create a 30-Day Challenge," *Thrive Global blog*, May 11, 2021, https://thriveglobal.com/stories/how-to-create-a-30-day-challenge-and-why-you-should/

9. http://www.mtbaldylodge.com/

10. Liz Barney, "Bethany Hamilton: Surfing With Only One Arm Isn't as Hard as Beating the Stigma," *The Guardian*, August 25, 2016, https://www.theguardian.com/sport/2016/aug/25/bethany-hamilton-surfing-espy-award

11. Don Grigware "Singing Coach to the Stars Marge Rivingston Talks Bout Her New Book and the Joys of Her Profession" *Broadway World, Los Angeles*, April 21, 2010, https://www.broadwayworld.com/los-angeles/article/Singing-Coach-to-the-Stars-Marge-Rivingston-Talks-About-Herself-and-the-Joys-of-Her-Profession-20010101

STOP CIRCLING

12. Christine Nishiyama, "Online Classes Don't Work," *Might Could blog*, https://might-could.com/essays/online-classes-dont-work/#:~:text=Udemy%20reports%20that%20the%20average,any%20better%20at%20online%20classes.

13. Lindsey Vonn, *Lindsey Vonn*, https://www.lindseyvonn.com/en/about-lindsey/

14. Deborah Johnson, *The Summit: Journey to Hero Mountain*, (2021),https://www.amazon.com/Summit-Journey-Hero-Mountain/dp/1733348425

15. *Die Hard*, https://www.imdb.com/title/tt0095016/

16. Wikepedia Free Encyclopedia, https://en.wikipedia.org/wiki/Alan_Rickman

17. https://www.cordonbleu.edu/home/en

18. Julia Child, Louisette Berholle, Simone Beck, Mastering the Art of French Cooking, Volume 1: A Cookbook, (New York, Knopf, Random House, 2008), https://www.amazon.com/Mastering-Art-French-Cooking-1/dp/0394721780

19. "Our History," https://www.mcdonalds.com/us/en-us/about-us/our-history.html

20. "Peggy Rowe," Simon & Schuster, https://www.simonandschuster.com/authors/Peggy-Rowe/155690413

21. https://mikerowe.com/videos/dirty-jobs/

22. https://www.self.com/package/challenges

23. Melissa Urban, "Plan for Whole30 Success," Whole30 blog, https://whole30.com/whole30-program-rules/

24. Andy Frisella, "How to Take Complete Control of Your Lie in Only 75 Days," https://andyfrisella.com/pages/75hard-info

25. https://plannerpads.com/

26. Francesco Cirillo, "The Pomodoro® Technique," Work Smarter, Not Harder blog, https://francescocirillo.com/products/the-pomodoro-technique

27. Bronnie Ware, The Five Top Regrets of the Dying: A Life Transformed by the Dearly Departing, (Australia, Hay House, 2012), https://www.amazon.com/Top-Five-Regrets-Dying-Transformed/dp/140194065X

28. Simon Sinek, Start with Why: How Great Leaders Inspire Everyone to Take Action, (New York, Penguin Group, 2009), https://www.amazon.com/Start-Why-Leaders-Inspire-Everyone/dp/1591846447/

29. John Templeton Foundation, https://www.templeton.org/discoveries/the-psychology-of-purpose

PURPOSE EXERCISE PART 2

30 Disney Institute Team, Disney Institute Blog, October 23, 2018, https://www.disneyinstitute.com/blog/mission-versus-purpose-whats-the-difference/

31 Viktor E. Frankl, Man's Search for Meaning, (Boston, Beacon Press, 2006), https://www.amazon.com/Mans-Search-Meaning-Viktor-Frankl-ebook/dp/B009U9S6FI

32 Celeste Leigh Pearce, Phd, "Association Between Life Purpose and Mortality Among US Adults Older Than 50 Years", JAMA Network Open, May 24, 2019, https://jamanetwork.com/journals/jamanetworkopen/fullarticle/2734064?utm_source=For_The_Media&utm_medium=referral&utm_campaign=ftm_links&utm_term=052419

33 Mara Gordon, "What's Your Purpose? Finding a Sense of Meaning in Life is Linked to Health," NPR, May 25, 2019, https://www.npr.org/sections/health-shots/2019/05/25/726695968/whats-your-purpose-finding-a-sense-of-meaning-in-life-is-linked-to-health

34 Viktor E. Frankl, Man's Search for Meaning, (Boston, Beacon Press, 2006), https://www.amazon.com/Mans-Search-Meaning-Viktor-Frankl/dp/1416524282/

35 https://en.wikipedia.org/wiki/The_Ladies_Who_Lunch_(song)

36 https://djworksmusic.com/

37 https://goalsforyourlife.com/blogs

38 https://goalsforyourlife.com/womenathalftimepodcast

39 Marta Zaraska, "Boosting Our Sense of Meaning in Life is an Often Overlooked Longevity Ingredient," The Washington Post, January 3, 2021, https://www.washingtonpost.com/health/boosting-our-sense-of-meaning-in-life-is-an-often-overlooked-longevity-ingredient/2020/12/31/84871d32-29d4-11eb-8fa2-06e7cbb145c0_story.html

40 https://www.nursingbeyondborders.org/

41 Leo Holtz, Christina Golubski, "Addressing Africa's Extreme Water Insecurity," Brookings Blog, July 23, 2021, https://www.brookings.edu/blog/africa-in-focus/2021/07/23/addressing-africas-extreme-water-insecurity/

42 Mike Muller, Money Down the Drain: Corruption in South Africa's Water Sector, March 2020, https://www.corruptionwatch.org.za/wp-content/uploads/2020/03/water-report_2020-single-pages-Final.pdf

43 "Martin Seligman & Positive Psychology", Pursuit of Happiness blog, https://www.pursuit-of-happiness.org/history-of-happiness/martin-seligman-psychology/

44 https://en.wikipedia.org/wiki/Zig_Ziglar

45 "About David Green & Family," Forbes Online, https://www.forbes.com/profile/david-green/?sh=484bfb1c4ef0

46 Barbara Dana, A Voice of Her Own: Becoming Emily Dickinson,, (HarperTeen, 2009), https://www.amazon.com/Voice-Her-Own-Becoming-Dickinson/dp/0060287047

47 https://en.wikipedia.org/wiki/Lincoln_Logs

48 Dr. Howard Markel, "How the Tylenol Murders of 1982 Changed the Way We Consume Medication," PBS News Hour, September 29, 2014, https://www.pbs.org/newshour/health/tylenol-murders-1982

49 "Facts + Statistics: Pet Ownership and Insurance," Insurance Information Institute, https://www.iii.org/fact-statistic/facts-statistics-pet-ownership-and-insurance

50 Associated Press, "450 Turkish Sheep Leap to Their Deaths," Fox News Live, January 13, 2015, https://www.foxnews.com/story/450-turkish-sheep-leap-to-their-deaths

51 "Elizabeth Gaskell Biography," The Gaskell Society, https://gaskellsociety.co.uk/elizabeth-gaskell/

www.ingramcontent.com/pod-product-compliance
Lightning Source LLC
Chambersburg PA
CBHW071243070526
44583CB00017B/2304